AF903590

"I am delighted that the popular Kiasunomics *series has returned for a third edition. As before, the authors — Professor Sumit Agarwal, Associate Professor Ang Swee Hoon, and Professor Sing Tien Foo — draw on the latest economics research to cast insights into contemporary issues of the day, such as climate change, fintech, and not least the perennial topic of property prices. Written in the same accessible, conversational style, these essays demonstrate, once again, how economic understanding can elucidate the changes happening in our society, and provide a sound basis for choices and actions."*

Professor Tan Eng Chye
President, National University of Singapore

"I enjoyed Kiasunomics 1 *and 2, and am delighted with the publication of* Kiasunomics 3, *and more importantly, that the authors have chosen the topical issues of the day like climate change. Tien Foo, Sumit and Swee Hoon have again brilliantly translated very complex urban economic issues into readable stories that will bring home important messages to a much wider audience than just experts and specialists. I would get my grandchildren to read these books. We pin our hopes for the future on them, and* Kiasunomics *has provided a way to stoke their curiosity and equip them with the knowledge to tackle the big challenges that they will face."*

Khoo Teng Chye
Chairman, Management Board of Institute of Real Estate and Urban Studies (IREUS)
Professor (Practice), Director, NUS Cities, College of Design and Engineering
National University of Singapore

"This is the third book in the phenomenally well-received Kiasunomics *series written in the same easy-to-read, story-telling style to explain abstract economic principles. The authors have again successfully demonstrated that the results of rigorous academic research translated into layman language and illustrated with examples applicable to the everyday life of Singaporeans have a much wider appeal. Readers can easily relate to the wide-ranging topics covered in the book to their daily experiences."*

Dr Seek Ngee Huat
Chairman, GLP Capital Partners
Provost's Chair Professor (Honorary), Department of Real Estate, Business School
National University of Singapore

Kiasunomics© 3

Economic Insights for Everyday Life

Kiasunomics© 3

Economic Insights for Everyday Life

Sumit Agarwal

Ang Swee Hoon

Sing Tien Foo

National University of Singapore, Singapore

World Scientific

NEW JERSEY • LONDON • SINGAPORE • BEIJING • SHANGHAI • HONG KONG • TAIPEI • CHENNAI • TOKYO

Published by

World Scientific Publishing Co. Pte. Ltd.
5 Toh Tuck Link, Singapore 596224
USA office: 27 Warren Street, Suite 401-402, Hackensack, NJ 07601
UK office: 57 Shelton Street, Covent Garden, London WC2H 9HE

National Library Board, Singapore Cataloguing in Publication Data
Name(s): Agarwal, Sumit, 1970– | Ang, Swee Hoon, author. | Sing, Tien Foo, author.
Title: Kiasunomics©3 : economic insights for everyday life / Sumit Agarwal, Ang Swee Hoon, Sing Tien Foo , (National University of Singapore, Singapore).
Other Title(s): Economic insights for everyday life
Description: Singapore : World Scientific Publishing Co. Pte. Ltd., [2024]
Identifier(s): ISBN 978-981-12-8345-1 (hardback) | 978-981-12-8393-2 (paperback) | 978-981-12-8346-8 (ebook for institutions) | 978-981-12-8347-5 (ebook for individuals)
Subject(s): LCSH: Economics--Singapore--Psychological aspects. | Consumer behavior--Singapore.
Classification: DDC 330.95957--dc23

British Library Cataloguing-in-Publication Data
A catalogue record for this book is available from the British Library.

Copyright © 2024 by World Scientific Publishing Co. Pte. Ltd.

All rights reserved. This book, or parts thereof, may not be reproduced in any form or by any means, electronic or mechanical, including photocopying, recording or any information storage and retrieval system now known or to be invented, without written permission from the publisher.

For photocopying of material in this volume, please pay a copying fee through the Copyright Clearance Center, Inc., 222 Rosewood Drive, Danvers, MA 01923, USA. In this case permission to photocopy is not required from the publisher.

For any available supplementary material, please visit
https://www.worldscientific.com/worldscibooks/10.1142/13598#t=suppl

Desk Editor: Jiang Yulin
Design and layout: Loo Chuan Ming

Printed in Singapore

Contents

Foreword

Tien Foo, Sumit and Swee Hoon's latest instalment in the *Kiasunomics* series presents day-to-day issues in interesting ways, drawing on deep research to offer interdisciplinary insights such as the correlation between rising sea levels and fluctuating property prices, and the impact of mobile payments on business creation. The *Kiasunomics* series makes economics fun and accessible, and I hope it inspires readers to contemplate why economics matters in today's world and how it influences the Singaporean way of life.

As I studied economics in university, the topics discussed in *Kiasunomics* are of special significance to me. Universities and academia are the brain trust of societies. When Government agencies and researchers work closely together to strengthen our mutual interests, we can generate impact beyond the academic domain, ignite ideas for problem-solving in a complex world, and calibrate policy innovations to address our efforts in areas such as education, information, housing models, and healthcare.

I am heartened by Tien Foo, Sumit and Swee Hoon's decision to donate the royalty proceeds from the *Kiasunomics* series to bursaries and scholarships, which will undoubtedly make a meaningful difference for many students in Singapore. I would also like to thank Tien Foo, Sumit and Swee Hoon for their efforts in expanding the sphere of Singapore-centric research, and I look forward to their continued contributions and perspectives in studying Singapore.

Chan Chun Sing
Minister for Education

Acknowledgments

Our thanks to our research collaborators who help make research meaningful:

ARARAL Eduardo
BASU Debarati
CHEN Yanying
CHENG Shih-Fen
CHIA Liu Ee
CHUA Yeoh Hwee
DAI Fangzhou
DENG Yongheng
DIAO Mi
FAN Mingxuan
FAN Yi
FAN Ying
GHOSH Pulak
GU Quanlin
HUANG Peiying
LI Jing
LI Qiang
LUO Chenxi
McMILLEN Daniell P.
PAREEK Bhuvanesh
QIAN Wenlan
QIN Yu
REN Yuan
RUAN Tianyue
SONG Changcheng
SULTANA Mahanaaz
TAN Poh Lin
TAN Weiqiang
TAN Yi Jin
TAN-SOO Jie-Sheng
TSAI Hsin Tien
WANG Yonglin
YEUNG Bernard
ZHAN Changwei
ZHANG Jian
ZHANG Xiaoyu
ZHANG Yunqi
ZHENG Huanhuan
ZOU Xin
ZOU Yiheng

Our heartfelt appreciation also extends to the organisations who generously shared their data with us so that research can be conducted to benefit the society.

The talented staff at World Scientific – Chua Hong Koon and Jiang Yulin – deserve praise for their roles in shaping this book and the series.

We also thank the staff from the External Relations and Corporate Communications offices at NUS Business School for their support.

Finally, our overriding debt continues to be our families, who provided the time, support, and inspiration for our research and preparation of this book.

Note from the Authors

- The Singlish term *kiasu* means "scared to lose."
- Some of the research findings presented in the book are from SSRN (Social Science Research Network) working papers. Readers without full access to the SSRN working papers can email any of the authors for a copy of the working paper.
- Unless otherwise stated, values prefixed with simple dollar '$' are in Singapore dollar.

List of Acronyms

ATM	Automatic Teller Machine
BTO	Build-To-Order
CBCRR	Cross-Border Currency/Bearer Negotiable Instruments Reporting Regime
CCA	Co-curricular Activity
CEA	Council of Estate Agencies
COVID-19	Coronavirus Disease 2019
CPF	Central Provident Fund
CPI	Corruption Perception Index
EAW	Estate Agents (Estate Agency Work) Regulations
FICO	Fair Isaac Corporation
GST	Goods and Services Tax
HDB	Housing and Development Board
LTA	Land Transport Authority
MRT	Mass Rapid Transit
MSG	Monosodium Glutamate
NUS	National University of Singapore
PIR	Price-to-Income Ratio
PM	Prime Minister
QR	Quick Response
REALIS	Real Estate Information System

SAI	Space-Adding Item
SLR	Sea Level Rise
STRO	Suspicious Transaction of Reporting Office

Introduction

After the encouraging feedback and success of *Kiasunomics* and *Kiasunomics 2* (K1 and K2 for short), we were heartened that people were interested in learning how to make better decisions. They were curious about our research and wanted to explore more in understanding their own behavior when it comes to making financial decisions so that they can make smarter choices. Indeed, this was what we wanted our research to be – relevant and impactful to the general public in their daily lives.

In our talks about the research featured in K1 and K2 at book festivals, libraries, conferences, companies and podcasts, research findings were brought to life that highlighted common and yet not obvious mistakes we make in our everyday lives. The books were also featured in newspapers and magazines, as well as discussed over the radio. We are deeply thankful to those who supported us and showed us that our research is meaningful. We are only too happy to bring our research closer to the general public.

In *Kiasunomics 3* (K3), we extended our sharing of research and decided to make each chapter standalone so that readers can pick and choose to read any chapter in any sequence. We want to reach out to time-challenged readers by having each chapter written in a crispier manner for a quick digest.

The topics are varied and include some contemporary issues. We cover the impact of the Prime Minister's National Day speech on issues ranging from the global warming effects on property prices to the relationship between Build-To-Order (BTO) flats and marriage and divorce rates to money laundering in the property market. Also discussed are the effects of fintech, such as QR codes, on businesses and the effects of data breaches on online shopping behavior. Have you ever wondered how parental bankruptcy will affect children financially? Or how does air pollution, such as the haze, affect academic performance? These issues are also researched and shared in K3. Quintessential topics such as financial support programs for senior citizens, public transportation, and property matters are also covered in K3.

We hope the third book of this series brings further learnings as more areas of economic decision-making are explored and we become smarter consumers.

As with the first two *Kiasunomics* books, all the royalty proceeds will go toward bursaries and scholarships.

CHAPTER 1

Climate Change and Property Prices

Three friends – Xan, James and Lizzy – had just finished their Geography class and were heading towards the nearby McDonald's for lunch before going back to school for their CCA (Co-curricular Activity). During their Geography lesson, they had discussed how most of the land in Singapore has an elevation of no more than 15 meters above sea level, and 30% of the total land is less than 5 meters above sea level. And someone in their class mentioned that the Intergovernmental Panel on Climate Change predicted that the sea level could increase by 0.43 to 0.84 meters by 2100. In the worst case scenario, this could raise by up to 1.8 meters by the end of the century.

"Quite scary, isn't it? I didn't know we are so low lying. Given the crazy weather we've been seeing, Singapore may soon be flooded," exclaimed Lizzy, as they sat in the comfort of the air-conditioned fast-food restaurant, half realizing the mockery of the situation – that the use of air-conditioning was contributing to the climate change.

"I remember my parents talking about a National Day speech some years ago in which Prime Minister (PM) Lee Hsien Loong spent a lot of the time discussing climate change. It is certainly serious and the government is already looking at long-term measures. Given Singapore's topography, we are at risk because of rising sea level due to climate change," added Xan.

"*Aiyoh*! I live in a terrace," said James. "Wouldn't that be low lying? My house is likely to be flooded compared to high-rise HDB flats and condos. Oh no! How, ah? I don't know how to swim well."

Everyone laughed. While personal safety came first, the three teenagers were also keenly aware of the impact of rising sea levels on property prices. In many Asian cultures, owning a roof over one's head has long been something everyone aims to achieve. Singaporeans are no different. In fact, houses form a significant portion of total assets – 42% to be exact. Compared to other financial assets, properties are vulnerable to climate-related risks. Hence, there is a real concern about how household wealth will be affected by climate change.

"Let's google and see," said a calm and thoughtful Xan.

"Hey look. There's this article here about Singapore's sea level rise (SLR). It says that these researchers from the National University of Singapore (NUS) took the topography map and digitized it to identify the SLR-prone areas that were highlighted during the PM's speech.

"They also obtained detailed transaction records of private and public housing. Properties in the SLR areas are in what is called the Treatment Group; and those outside SLR areas but within a 500-meter radius away from SLR-prone areas, are in the Control Group. So, they can compare vulnerable properties versus adjacent but less vulnerable properties. Look here. These are the digitized maps."

Both figures show the digitized maps of SLR areas (in blue) and property transactions. Each dot represents one single block that may include multiple property transactions. Transactions in the SLR areas are

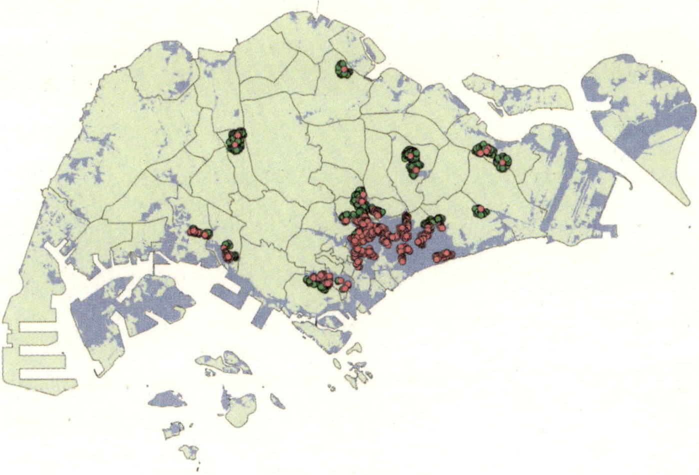

Private Properties

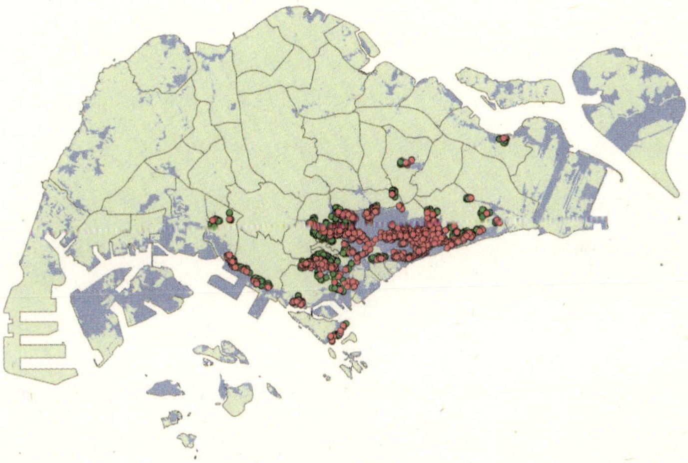

Public Properties

identified as the Treatment Group (red dots), while transactions outside the SLR areas but within the 500-meter buffer are in the Control Group (green dots).

"Wait, wait, wait . . . where's my terrace house?" said James as he peered closer at Xan's laptop. "*Heng ah*! Not in a low-lying area."

Xan promptly gave James a slap on the back of his head.

"Ouch!" yelped James.

"Guys, stop it. Let's see what the researchers found," said Lizzy, with a look of feigned despair at her classmates' antics.

"Look . . . there are several findings. First, prices of HDB flats in the Treatment Group declined after the PM's speech. These are the flats in the SLR areas. Prices of flats outside the SLR areas did not.

[A]fter the PM's announcement, these SLR flats depreciated, on average, by 3%.

"It says here that after the PM's announcement, these SLR flats depreciated, on average, by 3%. Hmm . . . if an average HDB goes for about $600k, that will mean a loss of about $20k. That can be hefty for some households. $20k can go towards paying utilities for several years.

"Oh, wait . . . the NUS researchers also found that the depreciation varied from 2% to 6%, and it wasn't a one-off thing. It persisted for a few years after the announcement. It's like these properties have been blacklisted."

"But look at the private properties in SLR areas," said Xan. "There was no price change. So, it seems that the PM's speech did not influence private property prices.

"And they did another study by expanding the 500-meter buffer to 2 kilometers for the SLR group of properties and observed similar findings."

"Interesting. Is the effect the same for older and newer flats? I would think older flats are more affected," asked James.

"Let me see . . . it says here that flats more than 20 years old and with a large area of more than 80 square meters experienced more depreciation after the PM's speech. So, you are right, James. But again, nothing was observed among private housing," explained Lizzy.

"Wait a minute . . . except for leasehold private properties. It's a lot of technical mumbo jumbo here that I don't understand. What is long-term discount rate? And what is long-term rental growth rate?

"Let me read to you what it says – 'the climate information shock could result in lower estimations of long-term discount rates'. Don't know what that means. But, here, it says that leasehold properties are less valuable compared to freehold properties, and hence, the impact of the PM's speech on leasehold private properties was more pronounced."

"HDB flats are also leasehold properties," added James.

"Yup, that's right. But, you know what? While the findings show that HDB flat prices are affected and private properties are generally not, it tells us something about the market, both the general population as well as the property industry," remarked Xan.

"It means that, before our Prime Minister made that speech on National Day, the property market did not fully factor in the impact of climate change on property prices. It was only when the PM announced the massive long-term investments into protecting Singapore from climate risks, then property prices, especially leasehold ones, were affected.

"So the PM's speech was a wake-up call to Singaporeans to be aware of the environmental impact on how attractive a property is, and hence, its price. Before that, we were still quite blasé about it, including those in the property industry."

[T]he PM's speech was a wake-up call to Singaporeans to be aware of the environmental impact on how attractive a property is.

"Yeah, you have a point there," agreed Lizzy. "The report also referred to Super Typhoon Mangkhut near Singapore in September 2018. It made landfall in Singapore and created a lot of floods. It said that the researchers compared property prices affected by the floods before and after the typhoon and found that this actual natural event did not affect prices as did the PM speech. That means that our government's announcements

Are older flats more affected than newer ones?
Yup. Those that are at least 20 years old depreciated more. But you know what? Prices of freehold private properties were not affected by the PM's speech.

So the PM's speech is a wake-up call to Singaporeans to be aware of the environmental impacts on how attractive a property is.
Perhaps those living in private properties are more aware of the impact of climate changes on their property and have factored this in the price.
But HDB residents may not have realized the consequences of the environment on property prices until the PM spoke about climate change.

are very effective in waking people up to the detrimental effects of climate change."

James nodded in agreement and continued. "Also, I think the findings are quite telling about the differences in the profile of public and private residents.

"I live in a private property. Now, I'm not being snobbish when I say this – maybe those living in private properties generally are in the higher income bracket with more wealth than those living in HDB flats.

"If that's the case, then might it not be possible that private housing residents, knowing more of what's happening around them, are already aware of the impact of climate changes on their property and have factored this in the price even before PM made his speech? Possible, right?

"On the other hand, it might well be that HDB dwellers did not realize the dire consequences of climate change on property prices until the PM talked about it in his speech. In which case, the speech came as a shock to them and what followed was an adjustment in prices.

"In other words, pre-shock private property prices already reflected climate change risks, while the HDB market did not price climate change until the speech."

Lizzy added, "I think there's also something to be said about the profile of private housing and HDB flat owners. HDB flats are public housing. Only Singaporeans qualify to own HDB flats by buying them directly from the government at a discounted rate. Hence, they are in Singapore for the long haul and invested in the future of the country. So, the impact of climate change is more pronounced.

"However, for private properties, while many are owned by Singaporeans, there is also a significant number owned by foreigners as well as permanent residents with foreign nationality. Compared to Singaporeans, they may be less concerned about future uncertainty as they can return to their home country and hence, the impact on property prices is weaker."

"Hey, we had better get back to school for our CCA," said Xan as he closed his laptop.

This discussion on climate change made Xan, James and Lizzy even more mindful of sustainability and not to be complacent about a living and healthy Earth.

WANT TO KNOW MORE?

This chapter is based on the following research:

Sumit Agarwal, Yu Qin, Tien Foo Sing and Changwei Zhan (2022), "Does Climate Change Affect Real Estate Prices? Evidence from Government Announcement," https://abfer.org/media/abfer-events-2022/annual-conference/papers-realestate/AC22P6008_Does-Climate-Change-Affect-Real-Estate-Prices-Evidence-from-Government-Announcement.pdf

CHAPTER 2

Flood and Spending

Claire was having an evening chat with her husband about his upcoming business trip to India. The weather forecast for Chennai, India, was thunderstorms. At the top of her mind was a recent conversation she had with her daughter Lizzy. Lizzy had told her about the growing frequency and intensity of natural disasters globally, and how climate change has affected property prices, specifically in Singapore.

The concerned wife wondered whether her husband's trip would be affected. Over the past several years, she noticed that more and more of her husband's business trips to India had been postponed because of heavy rains and floods.

According to the Centre for Research on the Epidemiology of Disasters, India is one of the top countries to experience natural disasters, especially floods. Natural disasters damage physical assets such as roads and stores, thus disrupting the supply chain in the delivery of goods and services. Other economic activities are also depressed, such as factories halting production because of damaged equipment. Even work from home is curtailed because most things are damaged. So, while disasters cause prices to increase, there is also a corresponding reduction in income. In short, livelihood is distressed from such natural occurrences.

Claire thought to herself, "How do they cope with these disasters? Besides having to clean out the mess caused by flood water, I wonder how they can even get basic supplies like food and clean water. And even having to repair damaged roofs and floors . . . I wouldn't even know where to start if this ever happened to me."

While understanding how the society and its people persevere to pick themselves up and rebuild their lives after a disaster, it is also crucial to understand how businesses change their prices and how households respond economically in their consumption. This informs us how to be economically resilient when a disaster strikes.

"Hey, dear, I saw on my iPhone that the weather in Chennai is torrential rain for the next two weeks. Is your trip still on?" Claire asked her husband. She felt uncomfortable with her husband's frequent travels, especially given the unpredictable overseas weather conditions.

"It is a go until my company says 'No,'" responded Arnie.

"What if there's severe flooding? It happened before, right?" asked his wife.

Seeing that Claire was interested in the floods in India, Arnie took this opportunity to enlighten her about how the Indians reacted to the floods, especially the one that occurred in Chennai in 2015.

"Unlike developed countries such as Japan and the United States, India has very low disaster-related housing insurance. This means Indians are particularly vulnerable when there is a natural disaster. And India is not short of natural disasters.

"In November to December of 2015, there was this huge flood in

Chennai, the capital of Tamil Nadu. It was during the northeast monsoon season.

"Whoa! The rain was torrential and the floods were unprecedented. It was one of the most damaging disasters throughout the world. More than 500 lives were lost and damage amounted to over US$14 billion. It was so bad that India's oldest newspaper, *Hindu*, that had been publishing daily since 1878, had to stop printing for the first time in its history. Incredible!

"But how the Chennai people responded economically to the worst flood they have ever had was quite remarkable.

"As to be expected, the flood disrupted the supply chain and reduced the supply of goods and services. Hence, prices increased. We can say that the Chennaiites experienced a price shock. So, what do you think their reaction would be?"

[T]he flood disrupted the supply chain and reduced the supply of goods and services. Hence, prices increased.

"Buy less?" Claire hazarded a guess.

"That's what most would think. On the contrary, they bought more. Sales quantity went up and so did sales revenue," said Arnie.

"Why? Because people started to hoard.

"What kinds of products did they hoard? Essentials.

"Why? Because they were uncertain about the future supply of such goods during the flood," said Arnie as he ticked off his points on his fingers.

"*Hah* . . . that's what I would do too. I'm *kiasu* but I didn't know Indians are *kiasu* too! If I know there'll be heavy rain coming for the next few weeks with a high possibility of flood, I will stock up on essential items, and build shelves way above the ground to keep the food dry," responded Claire.

Arnie continued, "But after the flood, the supermarkets in Chennai lowered their prices. This boosted more sales. But remember that Sales Revenue = Sales Quantity x Price. Because price declined but quantity increased, sales revenue remained unchanged.

"For non-essential items, they displayed what economists call high price elasticity of demand. People were not as interested in buying these items during a natural disaster. Since these items were discretionary, people wouldn't buy when there was an increase in price. However, when there is a reduction in price, demand goes up. So, in order to increase sales revenue, businesses selling these items would rather cut than increase prices. This mitigated the possibility that the flood reduced consumption through increasing prices of goods."

"But what about furniture or rice cookers that needed to be replaced as they were damaged by the flood?" asked Claire.

"Ah . . . these are durable but visible products that are essential," explained Arnie. "Others include floor and roof materials. The negative effect of the flood on demand for these products was less pronounced, and this did not vary by income.

"Since we're talking about income, let me tell you about income shock. Indians from different employment-income backgrounds responded differently. When there's a flood, shops and factories close early or did not open at all. So, for those who were on hourly- or daily-rated wages, which were usually the low-income earners, their income was adversely affected. So were street vendors as they suffered an income loss because of contracted economic activities.

"Contrast that with salaried people who receive regular salaries regardless of weather conditions. Their income remained stable.

"Not surprisingly, their reactions to how much they cut down their expenditure were different. Salarymen reduced their consumption less compared to low-income earners, both during and after the flood. This means that those whose income was badly hit by the flood accounted for most of the reduced consumption.

"Moreover, when the flood came, the Chennaiites switched to online spending. Onsite spending went down a lot more than online spending. But when the flood was over, store sales recovered."

[W]hen the flood came, the Chennaiites switched to online spending.

"But it's really quite heart wrenching, isn't it? To see how their lives were turned topsy-turvy by a calamity that was unpredictable and beyond their control?" said Claire.

"Yes, but financial lessons were learnt," said Arnie. "Financial liquidity is paramount during such times to pay for expenses.

"The Chennaiites used credit cards, took additional loans or cashed out on existing wealth to tide over their expenses. In this instance, less liquid assets such as stocks, gold and fixed deposits were too illiquid to provide timely liquidity to cover expenses incurred because of the flood. Savings was important, especially liquid assets that could be converted easily into cash to pay for such unforeseen expenses. So, savings bonds were good."

"Savings and having them in liquid assets are key during such times," agreed Claire. "We should remember to inculcate these practices in Lizzy."

WANT TO KNOW MORE?

This chapter is based on the following research:

Sumit Agarwal, Pulak Ghosh and Huanhuan Zheng (2021), "Consumption Response to a Natural Disaster: Evidence of Price and Income Shocks from Chennai Flood," https://papers.ssrn.com/sol3/papers.cfm?abstract_id=3777641

CHAPTER 3

Air Pollution and Academic Scores

"Mummy, we had an extremely interesting lesson today," said an excited Lizzy. It was quite unusual for Lizzy, as a teenager, to volunteer information about school to her mum. Claire was pleasantly surprised and thrilled at the opportunity to have more spontaneous discussion with her daughter.

"We learned about the impact of air pollution on public health," Lizzy said.

"We talked about the London smog in 1952. Then, my teacher told us about this study that found that mortality rates during high levels of air pollution are higher than previously thought. This study led the World Health Organization to revise the mortality impacts of air pollution. Besides mortality rates, my teacher also discussed studies on the impact of pollution on morbidity such as height of the population.

"But the most interesting study of all, Mummy, is the one on Singapore. In 1997, Singapore experienced one of the worst haze, due to Indonesian fires. My teacher said that researchers studied children who were *in-utero* during that haze. And guess what? Even after 17 years, these children, now teenagers, were 4 centimeters shorter than average! And this height deficiency translated to a 3.4% loss in income when they started working."

"Oh my! Air pollution can do that? By the way, what is *in-utero*?" Claire responded to encourage Lizzy to tell her more.

"*In-utero* means the length of time the fetus is in the mummy's uterus," explained Lizzy, as she felt a little smug that she could teach her mother something. "And there's more. My teacher told us about a recent study by a group of researchers from NUS Business School and the Lee Kuan Yew School of Public Policy. The researchers studied multiple cohorts of children who were exposed to different episodes of air pollution during their *in-utero* period and the impact of the air pollution on their 'A' level scores. Interesting, right?"

"Hmm . . . yes, that sounds interesting. I wonder how they were able to study the relationship," said Claire. She's quietly excited that her daughter is intellectually inquisitive.

"Well," continued Lizzy, "When applying for admission to NUS, students have to submit their 'A' level scores. The researchers used scores obtained from different groups of Singaporeans born between 1960 to 1997. Altogether, they studied over 466,000 students.

"Mummy, how many major air pollution periods were there between 1960 to 1997?"

"Eh . . . four?" was Claire's educated but hesitant response.

"That's right," said an impressed Lizzy.

"Singapore experienced haze in October 1977, April 1983, October 1991 and September 1997. The first two episodes were during Singapore's early development years and the latter two were when the country was already economically developed.

"For the first two haze episodes when Singapore's economy was still nascent, the researchers found that Singaporeans exposed to the haze *in-utero* had lower 'A' level scores than those unexposed. In turn, this lower score led to a 2.4% diminished chance of being offered admission into NUS.

Singaporeans exposed to the haze *in-utero* had lower 'A' level scores than those unexposed.

"If students had applied to one of the top NUS faculties for their study, their chances of being admitted were reduced by almost 3%. And this was the case for both males and females."

Lizzy continued. "The researchers also studied by residential type. Mummy, do you think living in an HDB flat or a private residence makes a difference?"

"I don't think so. Haze exposure is haze exposure, regardless of where you lived," remarked Claire.

Lizzy smiled because she has some news that is slightly different from what is expected.

"Exposed applicants from public housing were 3.7% less likely to be admitted into NUS," said Lizzy. "And 3.3% less likely to enter top faculties compared to unexposed applicants living in public housing. But the researchers didn't find this difference among applicants from private residences. This means that air pollution affected those living in public housing more than those living in private housing. Maybe those living in private housing can afford to give their children more tuition to offset the detrimental haze effects."

"Or, maybe, those living in private residences could afford to have air-conditioning as well as air purifiers to shield the expectant mother and her baby from the adverse effects of the haze," added Claire as an alternative explanation.

We learned in class today that air pollution not only affects mortality rates but even morbidity factors such as height.
Oh! That's interesting. I didn't know height is affected by pollution.
Well, researchers found that 17 years after the 1997 haze in Singapore, children who had become teenagers were 4 cm shorter! And not only that. It translates to 3.4% loss in income when they started working.
Their academic scores were also affected, Mum.
If they were in their mummy's womb when there was the haze, their 'A' level scores were lower than those unexposed to the haze! This affected their chances to enter the university.
But don't worry. In the recent haze episodes, there're air purifiers, air conditioners and face masks.
These protected people from the haze. And how well they did in their exams was not affected.

"*Wah*! Luckily, there was no haze when I carried you," joked Claire.

"But, Mummy, this was in earlier years before there were air purifiers," said Lizzie, rolling her eyes. "Is my mum paying attention to what I'm saying?" she thought.

"Mum, you haven't heard about the effects from the two more recent and severe haze episodes," said Lizzy impatiently.

"The researchers found no effects arising from haze on academic performance and admissions to NUS and the top faculties."

"Aahh . . . so my explanation holds! It's because, by then, Singapore is a much richer country and households can equip themselves with air purifiers, air conditioners and face masks to protect themselves against air pollution," replied Claire.

"I remember your father and I scrambled to buy air purifiers during the 1997 haze. They were selling like hot cakes and were out of stock in many places.

"Also, by that time, people were more knowledgeable about the harmful effects of air pollution than in the 70s and 80s. The Singapore government was publishing daily air pollution indices and sending reminders to the public to stay at home and not risk going out. So, Singaporeans have become more aware of the adverse effects of air pollution and took better care of their well-being."

Lizzy nodded, "That's what my teacher said too. Although there are harmful effects of early-life exposure to air pollution, it can be mitigated with adequate protection."

WANT TO KNOW MORE?

This chapter is based on the following research:

Sumit Agarwal, Poh Lin Tan and Jie-Sheng Tan-Soo (2023), "Long-term effects of air pollution on Singapore's national university admissions," *Applied Economics Letters*, https://www.tandfonline.com/doi/abs/10.1080/13504851.2023.2177586

CHAPTER 4

Tracking the Pulse of Singapore Housing

Roy and Cal have been married for six years and lived in their HDB flat for five. The millennial couple has a young family with a three-year-old son. They may expand their family with another child, depending on their financial situation.

According to the public housing rules in Singapore, Roy and Cal are eligible to sell their flat in the open market. They have always envied their friends living in condominiums as the private residences afford quieter surroundings and come with facilities that the couple foresee that their young family will enjoy.

"Maybe it's because of the type of people living there," said Cal. "People in condos tend to be more upper class and maybe they know better how to behave. No turning on their TVs loudly late at night. Less domestic shouting. No hanging of dripping clothes outside windows.

"Maybe we should consider upgrading to a condo. Our HDB flat can give us some capital gains to help us buy a private property."

"I was thinking of the same thing," replied Roy. "It may be time for us to upgrade so that Ah Boy can enjoy the swimming pool and hang around with younger families. Our HDB area has hardly any kids the same age as him.

"Let me check to see what condos are available and near a school where we can enroll Ah Boy. We must also consider whether the new condo we get can hold its price even when there's a downturn."

Roy did some searching and found that there was an index developed to measure property prices. A real estate index must be neutral, independent and objective, and can be used to analyze economic health of the property market. Policy makers use indices to diagnose whether a market is overheated and whether any action is needed to cool the market. Home buyers take cues from published indices before deciding whether to buy a property or not. Developers and property sellers also use indices to set their selling price.

"Eh, look at this one that I found. This index captures over 370,000 transactions of private properties from 1995 to 2017. During this time, there were two episodes of booms and busts – the Asian Financial Crisis in 1997 and the U.S. Subprime Crisis in 2007," said Roy to Cal. He still

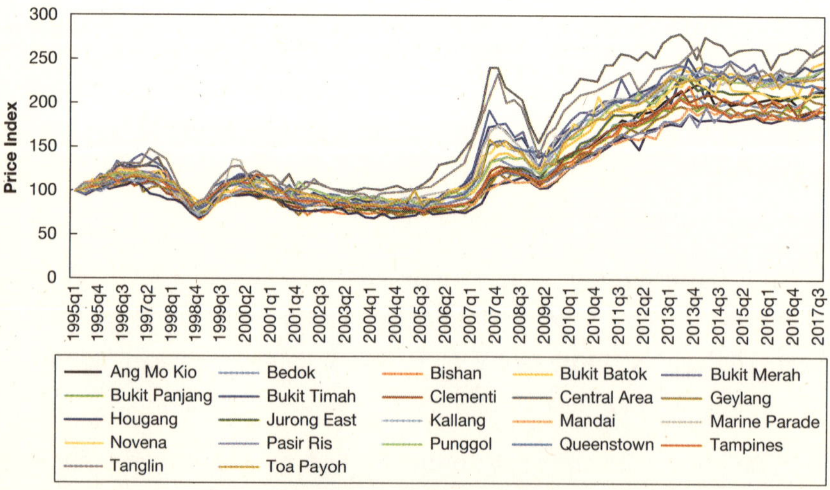

Price Dynamics in Some Regions

remembers the 2007 Subprime Crisis as it was such a big global event and his English teacher used it as a comprehension passage.

"Look here," said Roy as he guided Cal to a diagram he found online. "The high-price central region shows strong price increases while the low-price outlying areas experience a more moderate increase in prices during boom periods.

"There is also a heat map to show the price change," continued Roy. "*Wah*, look! The steepest increase in housing prices come from the central area coupled with a few pockets of smaller peaks between the Jurong East and Jurong West areas in the western region, and the areas around Bishan and Toa Payoh near the fringe to the northeast of the central area.

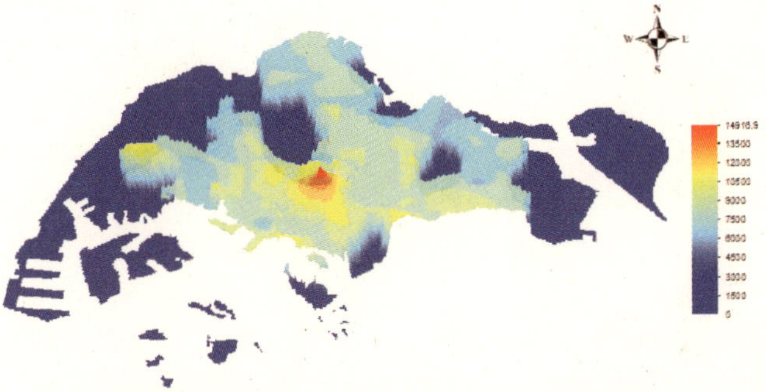

Singapore Housing Price Index 1995 1st Quarter

Singapore Housing Price Index 2017 3rd Quarter

Note: The difference in price is represented by the steepness and color of the surface of heat maps. The red-hot areas in the heat map represent the most expensive housing regions, followed by orange, yellow, green and light blue.

"The changing color and housing price patterns on the two heat maps reflect the urbanization process. The central region of Districts 9, 10 and 11 covering Novena, Newton, Grange Road, Tanglin Road, Orchard Road and River Valley Road, is the most exclusive and luxurious housing market with the highest rate of appreciation.

"Look at this one. It shows how much prices have gone up during each boom period. They break it down by region. The price is measured quarter by quarter to see whether it has increased. Light colors represent higher price appreciation.

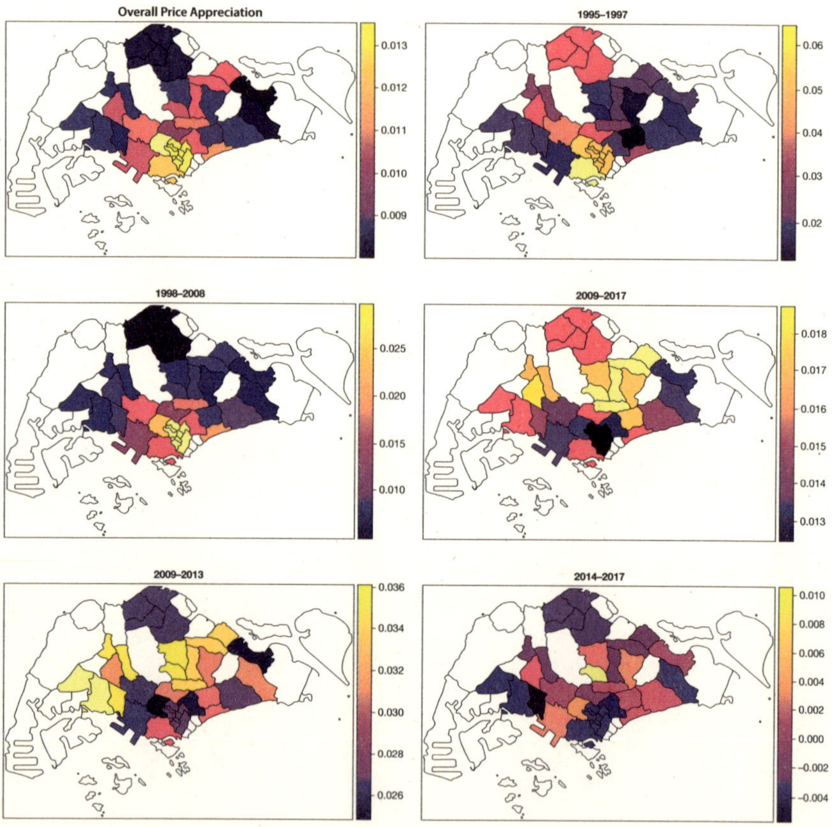

Price Appreciation Rates During Boom Periods

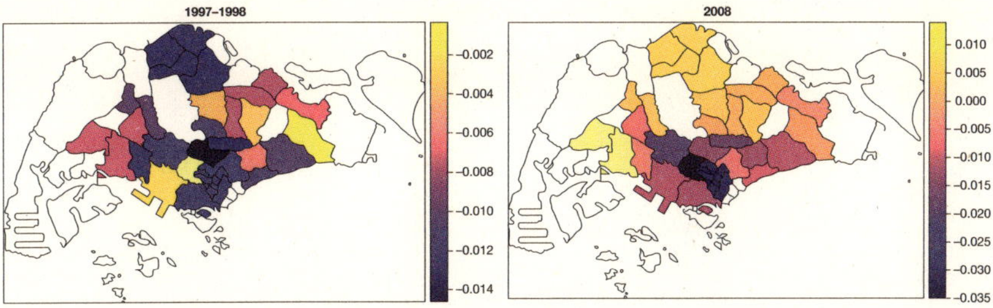

Price Appreciation Rates During Bust Periods

"When there is a boom, the average quarter-to-quarter appreciation rate is highest in the central area and the lowest in the northern and eastern regions. And during the downturn, the central area generally held its prices better."

"So, I think we should start by looking for a condo somewhere in the central region if we can afford to," said a concerned Cal, while making a mental calculation of how much savings they have and how much they can borrow from the bank given their current salaries. "It's a lot of money and we don't want to jeopardize our savings with a wrong decision."

WANT TO KNOW MORE?

This chapter is based on the following research:

Sumit Agarwal, Ying Fan, Daniel P. McMillen, Tien Foo Sing (2021), "Tracking the Pulse of a City – 3D Real Estate Price Heat Maps," *Journal of Regional Science*, Vol. 61(3), pp. 543-569, https://onlinelibrary.wiley.com/doi/10.1111/jors.12522

CHAPTER 5

Credit Card Rewards and Spending

While saving to upgrade from their HDB flat to a condo, Roy explored which credit card he and his wife should use to maximize returns. The market was saturated with credit cards offering different promotional rewards – cash-back incentives, dining discounts, collaborations with airlines and so on. It was difficult to compare one with the other. These incentives were presumably meant to save credit card users some money with the discounts or cash back. But he often wondered whether they may end up causing users to be penny wise but pound foolish.

He discussed this with Cal.

"Whichever credit card we choose, we must remember not to rely on the savings from a promotional campaign and use that as an excuse to spend more. We should just spend on what we need and not more," cautioned Roy.

"The concepts of 'needs' and 'wants' come to mind. Many people confuse the two. They think they are the same. But no. 'Needs' are essentials that people must have, while 'wants' are discretionary items that people can do without."

He recalled reading a newspaper article about a United States study on credit card spending that might well apply to Singapore. Singaporeans can learn a thing or two, and be more financially savvy.

The findings of the study were quite astounding.

Credit cards serve dual functions as a transaction instrument and a borrowing instrument. As a transaction instrument, credit cards are used to buy items. But if a cardholder fails to fully pay off the monthly balance on time such as making a minimum payment instead of a full payment, the unpaid balance incurs interest and becomes debt. In which case, credit cards become a borrowing instrument.

The study involved a major bank in the United States offering a 1% cash-back reward to incentivize its existing customers to use their credit card under a promotional program. The reward was by no means large. It was a relatively small reward – only 1%. Yet, despite its smallness, its impact was huge.

[T]hose who increased their credit card spending did not completely pay off the amount spent when payment was due.

On the spending side, the study found that cardholders who joined the promotional program increased their monthly spending on the card by $44[1], relative to those who did not join the program. This corresponds to a 32% difference. This means that a mere 1% cash-back reward could change people's spending behavior by 32%.

On the debt side, the researchers found that those who increased their

[1] All denominations in this chapter are in US$.

credit card spending did not completely pay off the amount spent when payment was due. Instead, it was converted into debt. On average, cardholders increased their debt by $75 or 8% per month after joining the program.

The greater dollar amount increase in debt compared to spending ($75 vs $44) means that card repayment declined not only for purchases due to the cash-back rewards but also on spending that is not related to the cash-back rewards. Such increased spending and debt persisted for the next 12 months with accumulated increases of almost $600 in spending and $900 in debt.

"Maybe they spent more on the card because of the incentive but spent less on other cards they have. So nett nett, they actually spent the same or maybe even less," conjectured Cal. She was thinking of how she would allocate her spending across her multiple cards to optimize the various promotions offered by the cards.

"Aahh . . . you mean whether there is a substitution effect?" said Roy, bringing back what he had learnt as an Economics graduate.

"The substitution effect refers to the change in demand for a product as a result of a change in the relative price of the product vis-à-vis that of substitute products. In this case, the 1% cash-back reward is like a discount for the credit card and hence, becomes more attractive than other credit cards without any promotion. The attractiveness would therefore lure a consumer to spend more on the promoted card and less on the non-promoted cards.

"I recall the researchers investigated and found that there was no evidence of a substitution effect. In fact, the overall balance on the other credit cards also showed an increase in spending per month. That means people just spent more on all cards," said Roy.

"That's not good news. You're supposed to save with the 1% cash back, and yet people ended spending more and, worse, increasing their credit card debt that carries a hefty interest rate of well over 20%. It doesn't make financial sense," Cal replied with a frown on her face.

"Maybe they overestimated their ability to pay off their bill when making extra purchases. They had initially intended to pay back in full but changed their mind when the bill came. And they seemed to ignore or did not realize the exorbitant interest rate on credit cards when they failed to fully pay off the balance. That's not good," said Roy.

Interest rates on credit cards are one of the highest, at least 20%.

"Oh . . . and that's not all, Cal," continued Roy. "Think about cardholders with outstanding mortgages and vehicle loans. They have long-term debts that require sizable monthly instalment payments. Such payments reduce their savings and disposable income. They are more liquidity constrained. The researchers found that, for such people, their spending and debt accumulation were higher than those without such hefty servicing commitments. They were already financially strapped, and the cash-back rewards made it worse for them because they spent even more with no ability to pay back in full."

"That's sad, isn't it?" said Cal. "It looks like those who need more financial assistance are spiraling down."

Roy nodded. "And the study showed that the financially sophisticated consumers were less likely to exhibit such irrational behavior. It's the financially naïve ones who spent more and accumulated more debt.

"The researchers also measured credit card utilization rate. This is the ratio of balance relative to available credit limit. The study found that those with more than 90% utilization rate, that is, people who max out their credit card, have accumulated spending of almost $2000 and accumulated debt of almost $5000. But those who have low utilization rate of less than 50% have much less accumulated spending and debt – only in the low hundreds. So, the more some people use their card, the more they accumulate their debt.

"Ultimately, such increased debt adversely affected their FICO scores.

In the United States, there is this consumer credit score called FICO which stands for Fair Isaac Corporation Credit Scoring System. It just doesn't work well for these consumers to have their FICO score lowered because of undisciplined and thoughtless spending."

"I bet the young ones spent more than the older folks," remarked Cal.

"Yes, I think that's what the study found. Those below 35 years old spent more and incurred more debt than those aged above 60 years old," replied Roy.

"So we had better drum it into our son from young to spend within his means. Remember, spend on needs and not wants."

"How about gender? Do women spend more?" Cal continued.

"I don't recall men and women to be different towards the cash-back rewards program. But married cardholders showed more spending debt than singles. So we need to be extra careful, Cal," said Roy.

"I think several things may be happening. First, there may be hyperbolic discounting and self-control issues. People discount present consumption over future consumption and tend to make choices that their future selves will not make, given the same information. They make impulsive decisions.

"Second, people have what economists call bounded rationality. We have limited capacity to digest all relevant information, and may end up making poor decisions. In the case of credit cards, the terms and conditions may be too complex for the average consumer, and they end up making suboptimal decisions.

We have limited capacity to digest all relevant information, and may end up making poor decisions.

"And worse still, some consumers may even justify their mistakes as financially insignificant or easily fixable errors. And so, the mistakes continue. They never learn from them."

We should be careful in how we spend. Spend on needs and not on wants.
A study found that in the U.S., people started to spend more on their credit card when there is a small incentive like a 1% cash back.
And they did not completely pay off the amount spent when payment is due. They became more indebted.
That's not good news. They're supposed to save with the 1% cash back.
Yet, people spend more and incur more debt. Interest on credit card is very high. They'll become even more indebted.
Exactly. It's irrational behavior. And those who are likely to fall into this trap are those who are less financially savvy.
We have bounded rationality. Our limited capacity to digest all relevant information may end up with us making poor financial decisions.

Cal added, "Maybe these cardholders double count or triple count their 1% savings. They know they saved, say, $50, and thought they could spend $50 more on something else. But that $50 savings excuse was used for several purchases. They might have forgotten they had already used up that savings.

"Anyway, these are takeaways that we should learn, and not get carried away in spending whenever there are such incentive programs."

WANT TO KNOW MORE?

This chapter is based on the following research:

Sumit Agarwal, Swee Hoon Ang, Yonglin Wang and Jian Zhang (2023), "Cash-back Rewards, Spending, and Debt Accumulation," *Working Paper*, National University of Singapore.

CHAPTER 6

Interest Rate Reduction and Financial Discipline

In anticipation of buying a private property, Roy and Cal did more research on mortgage loan rates. Besides asking friends about what they thought of the property market, they also searched online on interest rate trends as well as how people behaved regarding their finances.

Interest rates go up and down. For a long while, interest rates were kept very low but near the end of the COVID epidemic, interest rates started to rise. This however did not seem to curb property purchases in Singapore.

"It's scary how interest rates are increasing and we don't know when it will hit the maximum," said a concerned Cal. She is the one who manages the household budget.

"I'm sure it will decline one day. It can't go on increasing forever. There'll be a time when interest rates are too high to be economically productive. It will fall one day. Then history will repeat itself," assured Roy.

"We should be prepared regardless of whether interest rates rise or decline. Prudence is necessary. It might seem strange now with rising interest rates, but at one time, interest rates fell and it gave borrowers a pleasant surprise. But unfortunately, that did not result in the best financial behavior."

"What do you mean?" asked a curious Cal.

"This was in 2008," said Roy. "China had reduced the mortgage interest rate by 230 basis points, which was about a 36% rate cut. This was like a windfall to people who had taken out a mortgage loan on their house.

"The savings in paying less interest on a mortgage loan means that, on average, individuals with a mortgage enjoy more disposable income, constituting about 8% to 10% of their monthly income. That's quite a sizeable amount."

"Wow! That would be nice if we also have that extra money to spend," said Cal wistfully, hoping that mortgage rates in Singapore will also fall.

If mortgage rates go down, it also means interests earned on savings go down.

"Eh . . . but we need to be careful and not get carried away. If mortgage rates go down, it also means interests earned on savings go down. And whatever savings we get from lower mortgage rates should be spent on paying off the principal loan quantum than on discretionary purchases," cautioned Roy.

"Usually, people who apply for a mortgage loan are about 30 years old because that's when they settle down and begin to start a family, just like us! They are in their early stage of the life cycle and are more likely to face a higher level of mortgage debt burden.

"So if they have to service a high mortgage debt, then they are more likely to live hand-to-mouth than those with a lesser debt burden. They are cash constrained. But because of their higher debt, they will also receive a larger amount of disposable income due to the mortgage rate reduction."

"So that's good news, right? That the mortgage rate reduction will benefit them the most," said Cal.

"That's what you think. But guess what? That wasn't the case. On the contrary, there were signs of little financial discipline. After the announcement of the rate reduction, but before it was implemented, these people started to spend more on their credit card in anticipation of this 'windfall'. Their credit card debt increased by almost 11% when the rate decrease was announced, and most of the increased spending was on discretionary or non-durable goods.

"And after the rate cut was actually implemented, these cash-constrained consumers increased their credit card spending by a whopping 32% per month compared to those without mortgage obligations. Stunning!"

"Oh dear! This is indeed a lesson. Yes, we need to be financially disciplined. Otherwise, expenses can get out of hand and we will sink into more debt. Thank goodness there are these studies done in other countries that we can learn from instead of having to learn it the hard way by going through the financial hardship personally," said Cal.

WANT TO KNOW MORE?

This chapter is based on the following research:

Sumit Agarwal, Yongheng Deng, Quanlin Gu, Jia He, Wenlan Qian and Yuan Ren (2022), "Mortgage Debt, Hand-to-Mouth Households, and Monetary Policy Transmission," *Review of Finance*, Vol. 26(3), pp. 487-520, https://academic.oup.com/rof/article/26/3/487/6530353

CHAPTER 7

Marry for Love, or Love of House?

The Singapore government encourages home ownership. The Build-To-Order (BTO) scheme started in 2001 and expanded in 2011 to meet housing demands. Via the national housing authority Housing and Development Board (HDB), new public housing units are sold at subsidized prices only to Singaporeans who meet stringent eligibility criteria – there has to be a family nucleus and the family monthly income ceiling must not exceed $14,000.

Among the different types of family nucleus, the fiancé/fiancée scheme is the most popular among young Singaporeans as they get to obtain their first independent home at a more affordable price than those in the resale market or the private housing market. First-time buyers who buy these flats directly from the HDB, widely referred to as the BTO market, are given grants of up to $80,000. Moreover, as a young couple who have just started their careers, their income is unlikely to exceed the $14,000 ceiling compared to older couples who are more established.

Upon collecting their keys to the flat, they will need to solemnize their marriage within three months.

The Couple

John and Rachel met when they were studying in university. They had been together for two years. Now that both of them had graduated and embarked on their career, John suggested that they apply for a flat from the government. After all, they would need to wait four to five years before the flat would be available for occupancy.

"I think the timing is good. By the time we get the keys to the flat, we'll be in our late 20s or early 30s, just nice to get married. After another few years, we can start a family," added John.

"Moreover, we don't know whether we will be successful on our first try. We may have to ballot a few times. So, it's better to apply for BTO as soon as possible."

This being her first serious relationship, Rachel was idealistic about the relationship working out. Why not take the chance since there is balloting? Although her job required her to do some traveling, she was confident all would be well as they had been comfortable with each other for the past two years. They applied and paid only a non-refundable administrative fee of $10. If their application was successful, they booked their flat and placed 5% of the purchase price as downpayment.

But less than three years after applying for the BTO, their relationship got a little bit rocky. Besides some personal differences, Rachel's frequent travel meant that working out relationship issues was a challenge. Doubts began to set in about whether they wanted to spend their lives together. But the thought of forfeiting the 5% downpayment added financial consideration to the emotional strain. Despite these warning signs, John and Rachel went ahead and tied the knot.

The Research

A group of researchers from NUS Business School wanted to study the relationship between marriage and divorce rates, and application for BTO flats. They studied Singaporeans like John and Rachel aged 20 to 35 years old. This age bracket was chosen because 20 is the legal age for marriage in Singapore and 35 is the cut-off age above which singles can purchase BTO flats on their own. The researchers studied marriage and divorce rates, as well as consumption patterns of these individuals.

The figures below show the average age of married women and men across different types of residences. The data spans from 1996 to 2011 for resale HDB in either BTO or non-BTO blocks, while the BTO data starts from 2005 only when the first batch of BTO flats were completed for occupancy. BTO residents are much younger, by around five years, than residents in resale HDB flats regardless of whether they are in BTO or non-BTO blocks. Additionally, the age difference widens between BTO and non-BTO residents. This suggests that either young couples are more likely to choose to live in BTO flats or the BTO scheme influences early marriages.

> **[E]ither young couples are more likely to choose to live in BTO flats or the BTO scheme influences early marriages.**

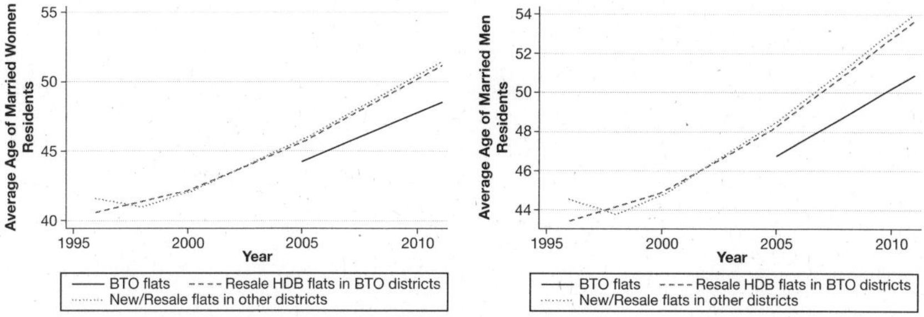

Average Age of Married Women and Married Men Across Residence Type

Similarly, the following figure shows a higher percentage of young couples under 35 years old living in BTO flats compared to other HDB residences. The difference increases along with time.

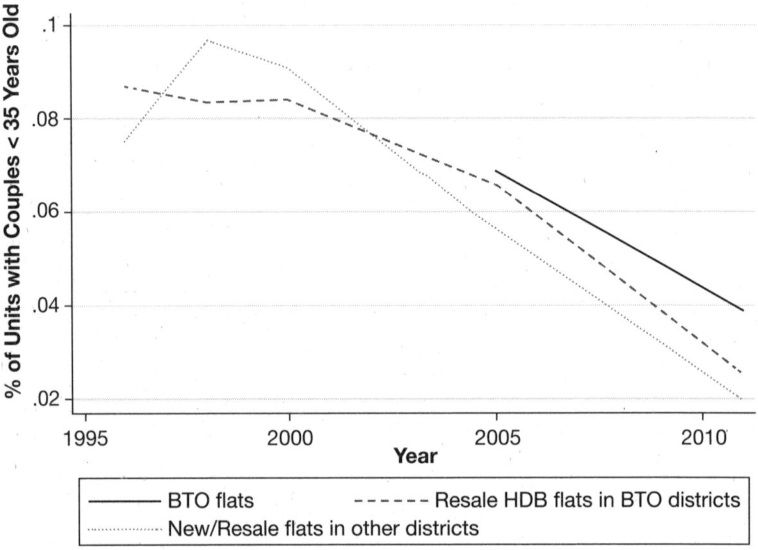

Percentage of Couples Aged Less than 35 Years Old Across Residence Type

Over the pre-2000 to post-2010 period, there was an increasing trend in marriage rate for females in the 25-29 age cohort from 45% to almost 60%, and for males in the 30-34 age cohort from 22% to 37%. The timeline coincides with the launch of BTO flats and its subsequent expansion. It is possible that in order to secure a BTO flat from competing applicants, more females aged 25-29 chose to get married to be competitive in the marriage market, while more men in the 30-34 age group chose to marry as they were more financially stable.

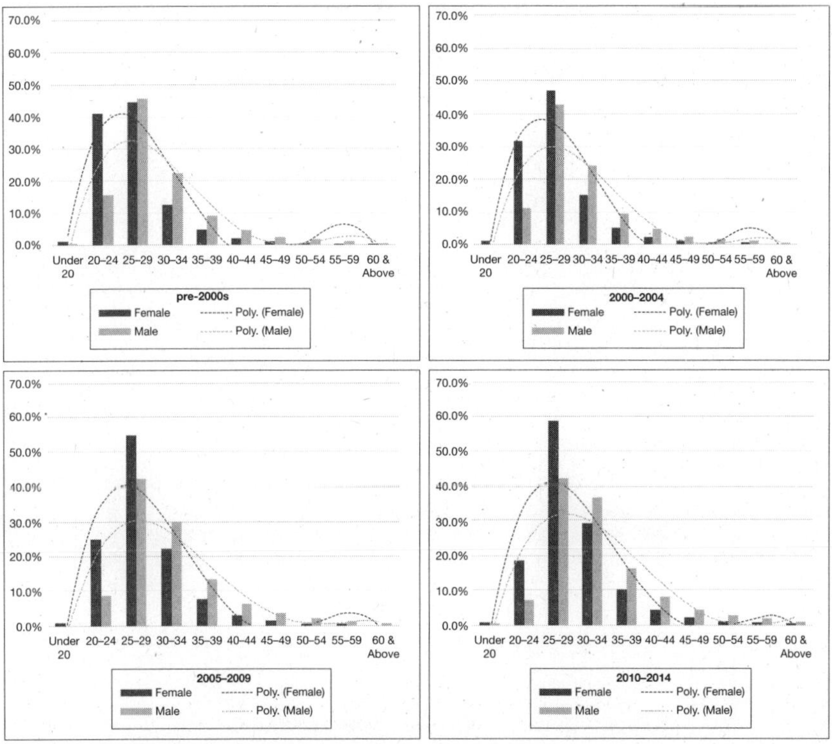

Marriage Rate Against Age by Gender and Period

There was a corresponding increase in divorce rate for females in the 30-34 age group from 4% to 7.2%, and males in the 35-39 age group from 3.5% to 6.3%. This trend also coincides with the timeline of the BTO scheme with a five-year lag compared to the marriage pattern. One possible explanation for the increase in divorce rates is that the BTO scheme might have rushed marriage decisions, which increase the likelihood of subsequent marriages.

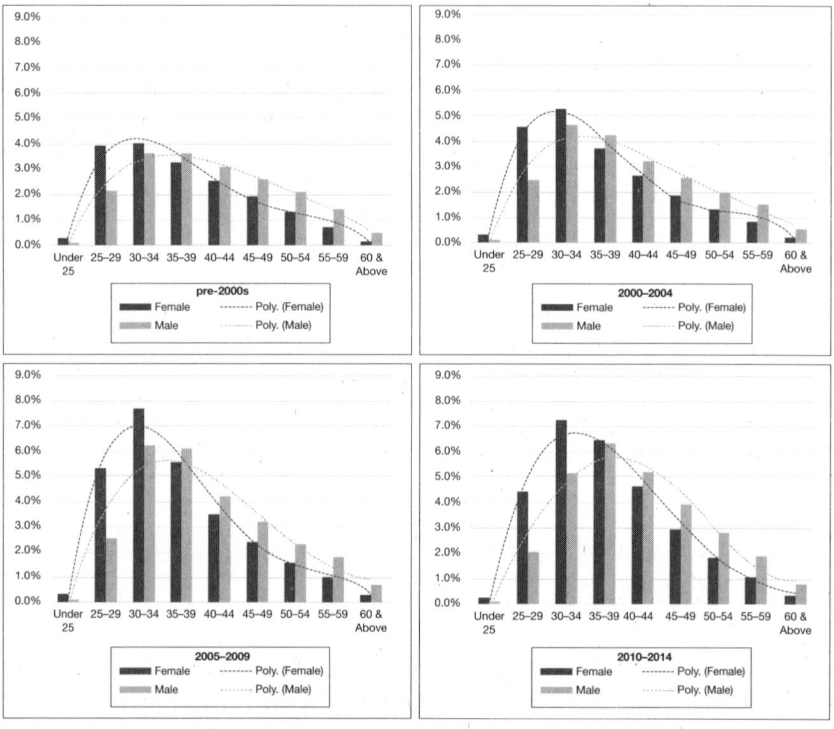

Divorce Rate Against Age by Gender and Period

There is evidence of fading marriage seasons. As a multi-ethnic society, Singaporeans of different ethnicities traditionally have different favorite months for getting married. Malays and Chinese like to get married in December, while June/July are less favored by Malays and April/August by Chinese. June is popular among Indians while September and

October are less favored. However, this dispersion across months for marriages became less pronounced from 2000 and especially after 2010, coinciding with the BTO expansion periods.

The researchers then studied the consumption patterns of those living in BTO HDB flats versus those in resale HDB flats. Compared to their resale HDB counterparts, residents in BTO flats have higher overall credit card expenditure by 6%. As BTO flats are newer than resale HDB flats, it might well be that they require more investments to kickstart – buying new furniture and fitting up their flats with new fixtures.

Interestingly, compared to singles in resale HDB flats, married residents of BTO flats have less monthly credit card spending by 7%. Such reduced expenditure comes mostly from necessity goods by as high as 19%. It is possible that BTO couples are cutting down on personal expenditure to save for mortgage payments.

Studying only married couples of BTO flats, the researchers infer that for young couples of 20 to 35 years old, the BTO flats are likely to be their first residences. The researchers observed that, compared to the year before moving into their BTO flats, married BTO residents born to parents living in private residences have a sharp increase (74% to 97%) in their monthly credit card expenditure, especially during the first eight months of moving into their new flats.

However, those coming from humble HDB roots spent less in their credit card expenditure, especially during the first five months of living in their new BTO flats. Their mortgage payments were almost halved compared to those coming from private residences. It is likely that the trade-off between personal consumption and mortgage payment

[T]hose coming from humble HDB roots spent less in their credit card expenditure, especially during the first five months of living in their new BTO flats.

is more pronounced among married BTO residents who had a humble start with HDB homes, at least for the first few months of moving into BTO flats.

To be comprehensive, the researchers studied singles above 35 years old who bought smaller 2-room Flexi BTO flats without forming a family nucleus. They found that they were three times more likely to buy BTO flats if they came from a humble start with HDB homes. But in terms of trade-offs between personal expenditure and mortgage payment, older single BTO residents were similar regardless of whether their parents lived in private or HDB residences.

All in all, it appears that the BTO scheme spurs early marriages. However, financial conditions of young couples may take a toll on the marriage, especially when there is less financial support from the family.

Post-COVID

The price-to-income ratio (PIR) is a measure of housing affordability. Pre-COVID, the PIR averaged 4.1 for 4- to 5-room BTO flats from 2001 to 2020. This is within a reasonable range of affordability, compared to 13.3 observed among 211 cities in 27 developing Asian countries. If various housing grants for first-time owners are taken into consideration, the PIR for BTO flats will be even lower.

However, post-COVID, there has been an increase in the average price of BTO flats and the rate of increase was faster than the increase in the median household income, resulting in BTO flats becoming less affordable. Moreover, the PIR is higher in mature estates and for bigger flats.

Despite the higher PIR, young couples gravitate towards BTO flats in popular mature estates, which saw oversubscription rates as high as 12.9 times. This means that only 1 in 13 applicants will be successful in getting a unit. But such mature estates are popular because of the location, amenities and proximity to public transportation and shopping malls.

With higher PIR, financial challenges will be exacerbated. Young couples need to save carefully for their mortgage payments even before they get the keys to their BTO flats. They should ensure that they are marrying for the right reasons – for love and not for the sake of being eligible for a BTO flat.

WANT TO KNOW MORE?

This chapter is based on the following research:

Sumit Agarwal, Yi Fan, Wenlan Qian and Tien Foo Sing (2021), "Marry for Love, or Love of House?" https://ideas.repec.org/p/arz/wpaper/eres2021_222.html

CHAPTER 8

Living Close to MRT Tracks

"Hey, when we look for the next house to buy, we should check how far the place is from an MRT station," said Roy to Cal.

"I know, I know," Cal said "Everyone's been talking about how houses near MRT stations appreciate in value.

"I want to be near an MRT station – all the conveniences associated with a variety of food and retail establishments that pop up near the stations.

"However, I don't want to be near rail tracks. I don't want to live with noise from train services. I heard that an MRT train running on an aboveground track can generate noise levels of 80 to 85 decibels, exceeding the acceptable noise level of 67 decibels for residential areas. There may also be vibrations caused by passing trains. *Aiyoh*! That would drive me crazy.

"And then of course, there are privacy issues. I don't want any Tom, Dick or Harry in a train to be able to look into my home when the train goes past. Yikes!"

"*Aiyah*! Don't worry. There are noise barriers to reduce the noise level by about 5 to 10 decibels," assured Roy. "LTA has been installing noise barriers. I remember there are three phases to this noise barrier project. But *yah lah*, the noise levels are still elevated although the barriers help in muting the noise.

"It's what economists call a disamenity. Living near an MRT rail track devalues property prices. Just like how properties near an airport are affected because of the noise from airplanes.

"Or remember the train from Singapore to Malaysia? Houses near train tracks are valued at a discount because of the noise from passing trains. But when the Malaysian transboundary train service ended, housing prices near the rail tracks rose by almost 14% because there's no more noise. The disamenity was gone.

"Let's see if I can find out more about how much being near an MRT track will set back the prices of these properties, and whether the noise barriers can mitigate the effect."

Roy did an online search and came across a study by the NUS Business School.

"Eh, dear," said Roy to Cal. "You are right. Living close to train tracks lowers the value of the property. There was this study by NUS that found that resale prices of HDB flats increase the further they are from above-ground MRT tracks."

"See? I'm right, eh?" said Cal, smiling to herself that she got this intuition spot on.

Roy continued. "These researchers are quite careful in how they studied the effects. Because being near an MRT station has its benefits, their study excluded properties within 400 meters of MRT stations. So the results were purely for flats that were less likely to benefit from proximity to MRT stations."

"So what did they find?" asked Cal. She's curious.

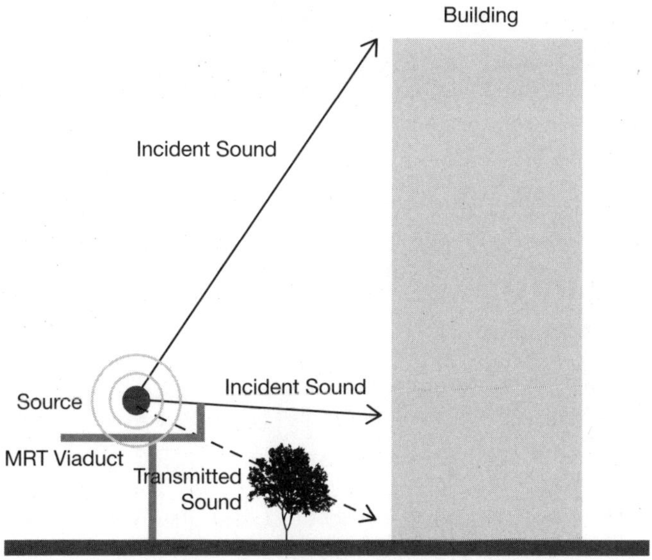

Noise Transmission Without Barrier

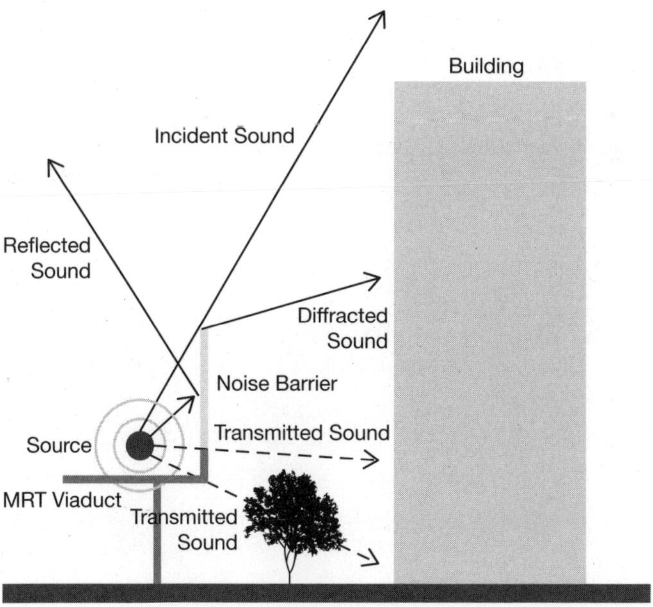

Noise Transmission with Barrier

"Hmm . . .," said Roy slowly as he scanned the article on his laptop. "They found that the prices of such HDB flats increased by 3% to 4% for every 1 kilometer increase in the distance away from MRT tracks.

[P]rices of such HDB flats increased by 3% to 4% for every 1 kilometer increase in the distance away from MRT tracks.

"But for flats close to the rail tracks, there was some good news. The noise barriers that LTA installed helped somewhat. When it was announced that noise barriers would be put in place, the disamenity effects dropped from 1.4% to 2.2% for every 1 kilometer decrease in distance to MRT tracks.

"After the noise barriers were completed, the disamenity effects were reduced by almost 5% for every 1 kilometer decrease in distance to noise barriers."

"What does 'disamenity effects dropped' mean? Too *cheem*," laughed Cal. Sometimes, she wonders why there are such terms that no ordinary person would understand.

"Ahh . . .," laughed Roy. "What it means is that, with the removal of the disamenity, which meant less noise, it translated to housing prices increasing by 2% and 3% after the announcement and completion of noise barriers, respectively."

[H]ousing prices increas[e] by 2% and 3% after the announcement and completion of noise barriers, respectively.

"So what does this mean in dollars?" asked Cal.

"Well, let's take Phase 1 of the noise barrier project as an example," explained Roy. "If we assume that each HDB block has 100 flats and there are about 1600 HDB blocks within a 500-meter buffer of the barriers, we take the average transaction price and increase it by 2.8% and add that up for all the flats. We find that the total value gain in property prices from installing the noise barriers is about $700 million.

"But we should compare that value gain against the cost of erecting the noise barriers to assess whether it is economically worth the while. Do you know how much we spent on the noise barriers? LTA reported the total costs of the three phases to be about $300 million. All in all, the benefits outweigh the costs. In fact, just based on the noise barrier project in Phase 1, the enhanced property prices of $700 million are more than the costs of all three noise barrier projects of $300 million."

"Eh, I know everyone says the price is sure to go up if you live near an MRT station. But I think there are also benefits other than price appreciation, right?" Cal asked.

"I read that the same NUS profs who studied the noise barrier effect also studied the Circle Line station effect," replied Roy. "They found that, with the opening of the Circle Line, MRT's share of travel went up. That, of course, is understandable. But interestingly, the use of private cars as a mode of transport went down by almost 7%, especially for residents living near the stations.

"For people living within 500 meters of the Circle Line stations, the average vehicle distance traveled went down by 38% compared to those living 500 to 1500 meters from the stations."

"So, that means for people living near an MRT station, not only do they enjoy an appreciation in their property value, but they also save by not having to use their cars that often or even not needing one at all," Cal said with a wink.

I don't want to live near the track. I don't want any Tom, Dick or Harry to see me at home. No privacy leh. And the noise. *Aiyoh*! How to watch TV or study? Surely, the property price will be affected.
This is called a disamenity. Living near an MRT track devalues the property. But don't worry. There are noise barriers.

Proximity to MRT tracks affects property value. But when the barriers were in place, housing prices increased by almost 3%.
In fact, if we add up the gains across all the flats, the total value added is way more than the cost of the barriers.

And if we live near the MRT station, I think I will sell off our car. We don't need the car as much. We will use more public transport and save.
When the Circle Line was opened, car usage went down by almost 40% among people living within 500 m of the station compared to those living farther away.

WANT TO KNOW MORE?

This chapter is based on the following research:

Mi Diao, Qiang Li, Tien Foo Sing and Changwei Zhan, (2023) "Disamenities of Living Close to Transit Tracks: Evidence from Singapore's MRT System," *Regional Science and Urban Economics*, Vol. 100, 103894.

Fangzhou Dai, Mi Diao and Tien Foo Sing, (2020) "Effects of New Urban Rail Transit Line on Individual Travel Mode Share: A Two-Dimensional Propensity Score Matching Approach," *Transportation Research Part D: Transport and Environment*, Vol. 89, 102601.

Fangzhou Dai, Mi Diao and Tien Foo Sing, (forthcoming) "A Two-Dimensional Propensity Score Matching Approach to Estimating the Treatment Effect of Urban Rail Transit Lines on Vehicle Travel," *Transportation*.

CHAPTER 9

Inflation Expectations and Lifestyle Change

"Roy, since we're not buying a bigger flat or a condo yet, I want to get that Louis Vuitton Neverfull bag," said Cal.

"I've been eyeing my first brand name bag for a long, long time. I'm quite tired of carrying the same old no-name bag. Anyway, the quality of brandless bags is quite poor and they spoil so easily."

"But I want to change our TV set," remarked Roy. "This old one is going to go bust soon. There's the occasional flicker and the color seems off. I kind of like the new Samsung OLED TV with its state-of-the-art technology for better picture and sound."

Conversations like this are not uncommon. With economic growth, lifestyle has changed. People aspire to own and enjoy better products. The basket of goods that economists use to measure inflation has also changed. Items that were previously not available, such as smartphones, are now considered necessities in many households.

As the standard of living increases, consumers are exposed to more varieties of products and at better quality too. Within the same product category, consumers may shift their spending to brands of higher quality. The no-name fabric handbag that they used to carry may have been upgraded to a brand name leather bag. This will lead to an upward bias in inflation expectations, termed as the upgrading channel.

Spending and Upgrading

A study by NUS used a dataset of consumer financial transactions to investigate whether there were, indeed, upgrading channel effects. The research team divided Singapore households into five quintiles based on income and observed what they spent on different product categories over a five-year period. The higher the quintile, the higher is the income bracket.

Product Categories	1st Quintile	2nd Quintile	3rd Quintile	4th Quintile	5th Quintile
Watches and Jewelry	8.1%	14%	12.4%	7.6%	6.4%
Entertainment	20.6%	12.3%	3.1%	-3.1%	-1.7%
Restaurants	-20%	-7%	5.3%	14.4%	16.7%
Apparel	-2.7%	9.4%	14.4%	16.7%	5.5%

Change in Spending on Various Product Categories by Income Quintiles

Roy's curiosity was piqued. "What do you think they found?" he asked Cal.

"I think people from different socio-economic brackets will spend differently," replied Cal.

"Well, the researchers found that there was a different rate of increase in annual credit card spending in different categories of products," noted Roy. "For luxury products such as watches and jewelry, as well as entertainment, they observed that, over time, there was a larger increase in spending among households in the two lower quintiles (1st and 2nd quintiles) compared to higher quintiles. This meant that people in such households were upgrading to buy more aspirational products.

[H]ouseholds aspire to upgrade themselves and spend more on products associated with economic progress.

"For apparel and restaurants, there was a larger increase in consumption among higher rather than lower income households. This meant that people in higher income households were spending more on high-end clothes and dining out. Together, the findings suggest that, across product categories, households aspire to upgrade themselves and spend more on products associated with economic progress."

Indeed, the research reported that while the average monthly spending by households remained relatively stable across quintiles, the researchers found that the index for measuring the quality of products bought fluctuates across quintiles. Specifically, there is huge variation between households from the 2nd quintile to 4th quintile, with the lower quintiles converging to the higher quintiles, suggesting that there is a tendency for these households to upgrade to better quality products over time.

Households with lower education, lower income and stay in HDB flats were observed to have higher inflation expectations and perceptions. The higher the education level, the lower was inflation expectations and perceptions. Singaporeans living in HDB flats reported higher inflation expectations and perceptions.

"How about women, especially married women?" asked Cal as she is mindful she belongs to that demographic group.

"Women and married individuals were found to have higher inflation expectations and perceptions," her husband answered. "Households with children at home (aged 18 years and below) also tend to have higher inflation perceptions and expectations. This is likely due to the type of products that these households might need to purchase because of the stage in their life cycle. For instance, for households with young children, they would need to purchase infant milk powder and diapers. This provides additional evidence for higher inflation expectations due to the changing composition of products by households.

"Those households with secondary school children at home experienced the highest increase in inflation expectations, probably due to higher expenses associated with schooling at this age."

Price Experiment

"The profs then did an experiment," continued Roy. "They gave different information to different groups of people. They showed people the prices of Häagen-Dazs and Walls ice cream – a premium (upgraded) and mass brand, respectively. There were three experimental groups, or three groups of people:

Group 1 saw prices of Walls in 2010 and 2019

Group 2 saw prices of Walls in 2010 and Häagen-Dazs in 2019

Group 3 saw prices of Walls in 2010 and 2019, and the price of Häagen-Dazs in 2019

"Everyone was asked two questions concerning their perceived financial well-being:

1. "Do you feel that you and your family are currently better off, worse off, or roughly the same financially compared to 12 months ago?"
2. "Looking forward, do you feel that you and your family will be better off, worse off, or roughly the same financially in 12 months' time compared to now?"

"The profs were interested in Group 3 where prices of Walls in 2010 and 2019 were given together with the price of Häagen-Dazs in 2019. They found that the additional information about the price of Häagen-Dazs ice cream in 2019 did not upwardly bias inflation expectations for Singaporeans who thought their financial well-being was not worse off, as much as it did for those who thought they were worse off."

"How then can Singaporeans reduce inflation expectations?" asked Cal.

"If Singaporeans are cognizant that their inflation expectations are driven by their own spending habits as they opt for upgraded products across different categories, then their expectations about inflation may be tempered," said Roy.

Rising Interest Rates

"Here's another concern. Interest rates have risen to a high level. With high interest rates, how can Singaporeans keep up with inflation? There are families with low combined take-home salary and with a mortgage to service and children's expenses to cover," wondered Cal.

"Well, I think for Singaporeans who are liquidity constrained and do not readily have cash in hand, they are more likely to borrow from banks for their major purchases. Servicing such loans will become challenging as interest rates rise," said Roy.

"Consider a family with a combined take-home pay of about \$3000 a month, \$1000 of which goes toward mortgage payment and another \$1000 for children's education, transportation and other necessities, and the last \$1000 for discretionary spending like dining out and clothes. They will be tapped out by the end of the month and will live from paycheck to paycheck.

"When interest rates go up, say from 1.5% to 3%, the debt service burden has essentially doubled. Singaporeans in the lower income bracket will find it difficult to service their mortgage payment."

"What can they do then?" enquired Cal. She is quite concerned about Singaporeans who may fall into this group and be stuck in a web of financial difficulties.

Roy replied as he raised pointing his finger. "Three options are available. First, they can default on their mortgage. This is not a pleasant situation and the relevant parties may want to consider some bridging alternatives.

"Second, they can borrow on their credit cards and take on debt to support current spending at the cost of future spending. This is also not desirable as the interest rate on credit card debt is significantly higher than most other debts.

"Third, they can cut down discretionary spending on such items as electronics, clothes and outside meals. Essentially, they have to tighten their belts."

Roy continued. "In Singapore, banks give a maximum loan of 75% of the house value. Home buyers are therefore likely to have drawn down their savings for the downpayment – savings that would otherwise come in handy when interest rates rise.

[M]any homebuyers have a tendency to buy bigger homes in anticipation of future housing needs. This means that, when interest rates increase, their debt service burden also increases by a bigger quantum.

"Additionally, many homebuyers have a tendency to buy bigger homes in anticipation of future housing needs. This means that, when interest rates increase, their debt service burden also increases by a bigger quantum.

"The scenario of rising interest rates may well change Singaporeans' perspective of buying bigger homes than what they currently

Dear, do you think we're spending more now as we've started to buy branded items? Do you feel we've upgraded?
Well, yes and no. While I can now afford better quality stuff, I also feel that things are getting more expensive. When I compare the prices of ice cream 10 years ago and now, I am aware that there is inflation. I also spend more because I buy higher-end products.

With interest rates rising, we need to be mindful of spending. Servicing our housing loan will be tougher.
I think we can manage. But what options are there for other people?

Well, cut down on spending on discretionary purchases. Just tighten the belt. If not, they can borrow on their credit card but this is not desirable. Or they can consider some bridging alternatives when it comes to loans. The worst case is to default on mortgage.

need. Buying the type of residence that best fits their current needs instead of a larger one means smaller mortgage payment that will give them the much-needed buffer for future rate increases."

"So perhaps we should re-think about what we want for our next house," said Cal after pondering over what Roy had just explained. "Maybe buying within our means and for current needs will be more prudent than buying a much larger one that may become a financial strain on us."

WANT TO KNOW MORE?

This chapter is based on the following research:

Sumit Agarwal, Yeow Hwee Chua and Changcheng Song (2020), "Inflation Expectations and the Upgrading Channel," https://papers.ssrn.com/sol3/papers.cfm?abstract_id=3559176

Sumit Agarwal, "Consumers Feel the Pinch of Rising Interest Rates," *Channel News Asia*, 22 February 2019.

CHAPTER 10

Water Consumption

"Lizzy, we need to be more careful in using water. Our water bill has been going up," said Claire to her daughter.

"Daddy also uses a lot of water. He's in the toilet for so long whenever he takes a shower," protested Lizzy.

"Yah *lah*. All of us need to be more mindful of how much water we are using," said Claire to both her daughter and husband. "Remember about sustainability. We need to protect the environment by not wasting water.

"We are fortunate to be living in Singapore where we get plenty of clean water easily. But elsewhere, some cities face water shortage given their growing population. So, there's rationing to conserve water usage.

"Prices of everything are going up. The Singapore government announced that there will be a two-phased 30% water price increase. If we use less water, the increase in tax is less and so we pay less."

The next day, Claire met her former secondary school classmates who had become friends. They had gone down different paths over the years. Some had carved out a successful career and lived in private properties, while others had other priorities and lived more modestly in HDB flats. They were discussing the announcement of the water price hike.

"When the announcement came out, I immediately told my husband to use less water, especially when showering. Turn off the tap when he is lathering and don't leave the tap running," said Nadiah, who lives alone with her husband. She has no children.

"I think we actually used less water already. We're training for when the price actually increases."

"*Aiyoh*! My husband and children aren't even listening," complained June. "We use a lot of water, more than the average Singapore household. Yet, it's like in one ear and out the other. I think the announcement has no sting on them. Maybe I have to wait until the price actually goes up, then they'll pay attention to how much water they are wasting."

Claire found this discussion fascinating. She had always wondered whether the price hike announcement would affect Singaporeans differently depending on their income and water consumption levels. Would people who use a lot of water be more sensitive to the announcement and start to curb their water consumption? Or, would they be more responsive only when the price hike took effect?

So, when the community center organized a talk on saving water, Claire thought she might attend to learn, not just how to conserve water, but also check if the price hike worked in discouraging water wastage.

The Community Center Talk

It turned out that the talk also discussed how Singaporeans responded to the announcement and the subsequent implementation of the price hike. The mere announcement alone resulted in a 3.7% reduction in household water consumption. An average household size of 3.16 persons consumes about 17.5 cubic meters of water per day. The announcement led to a saving of 3.7% or 6.65 cubic meters of water saved per capita per day.

The effect of the announcement varied by household type. The monthly water consumption averaged between 11.2 cubic meters for HDB 1- and 2-room flats and 20.5 cubic meters for executive flats. Households living in HDB flats, compared to private apartments, reduced water consumption by 5.8% after the announcement of the price increase. This 5.8% reduction translates to almost 10 liters of water saved per capita per day.

The announcement had more effect on households that used less water.

Interestingly, the effect of the announcement was not the same for everyone. The announcement had more effect on households that used less water. Households that used more water did not react to the

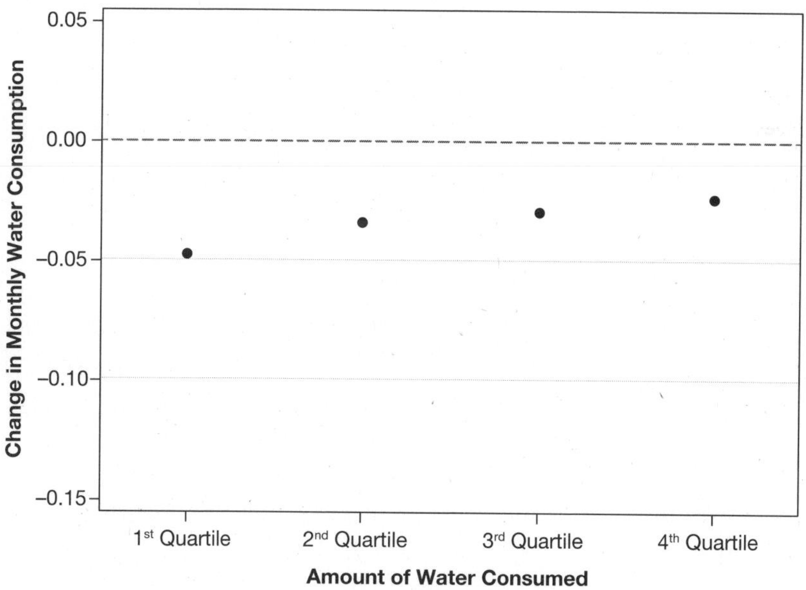

Effect of Announcement on Change in Monthly Water Consumption

announcement, i.e., they continued to use as much water as before. The effect did not vary by the size of HDB flats. This meant that, regardless of whether people lived in a 2-room, 3-room, 4-room, 5-room or Executive flat, how much they cut down on their water usage in response to the announcement depended on how much water they were already consuming before the announcement.

Claire thought, "This is like my friends Nadiah and June. Nadiah's family used less water and they cut down on water usage when the announcement was made. But June's family, who used a lot more water, seemed indifferent to the announcement."

However, Claire also learnt that Singaporeans' reactions were somewhat different when water prices were actually hiked up. When the price increase was implemented, it caught the attention of households that had been using a lot of water.

Unlike the announcement effect where heavy users did not appear to be affected, the price implementation effect was stronger for households that were heavy users of water compared to households that use less water, regardless of the type of HDB flat they live in. These high-water usage households became more sensitive to the actual price increase because they feel more pain from the actual price hike than the announcement of a price hike.

In general, the price hike resulted in 2.1% decline in water consumption.

This was also the case with the second price hike a year later. It led to a 2.8% reduction in water usage. And again, just like the first price hike, the impact of the actual price change was more prominent for households with higher water usage, leading to a larger adjustment in water consumption.

Claire also learnt that the average monthly water consumption was reduced from 17.3 cubic meters to 15.4 cubic meters for HDB flats, and 16.3 cubic meters to 14.3 cubic meters for private apartments.

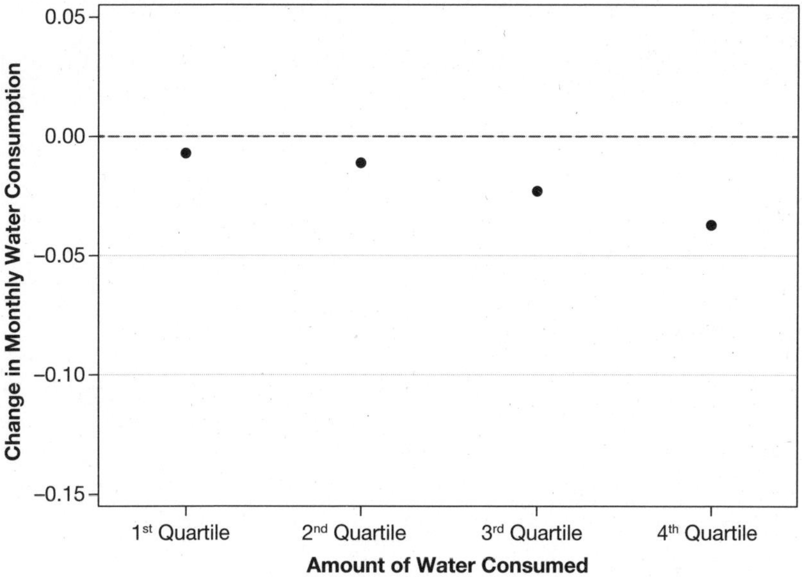

Effect of 1st Price Change by Consumption Level

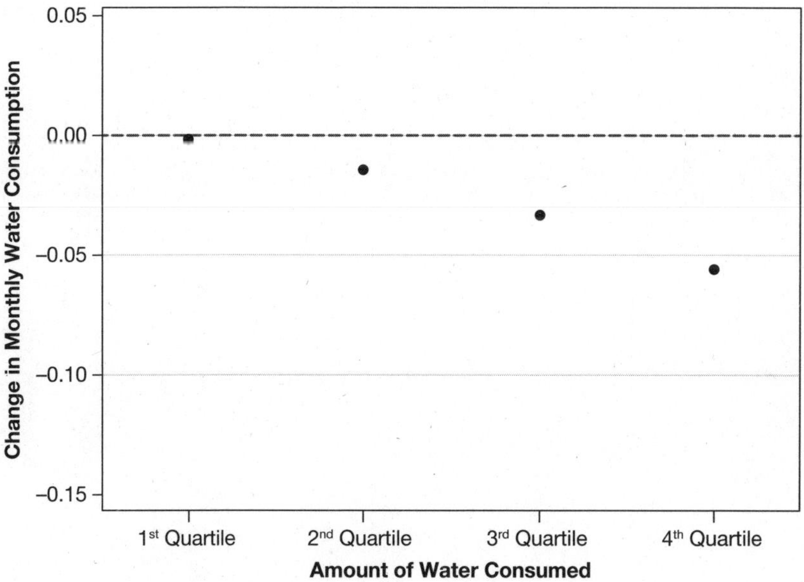

Effect of 2nd Price Change by Consumption Level

Claire thought that the increase in water prices curbed overall consumption whether through the announcement or during the actual price increase. Interestingly, different households had different reactions to the announcement and actual price implementation, depending on their level of water consumption and not because of their type of residence.

WANT TO KNOW MORE?

This chapter is based on the following research:

Sumit Agarwal, Eduardo Araral, Mingxuan Fan and Yu Qin, Huanhuan Zheng (2023), "The Effects of Policy Announcement, Prices, and Subsidies on Water Consumption," https://papers.ssrn.com/sol3/papers.cfm?abstract_id=4318217

CHAPTER 11

Are Women More Strategic Taxi Drivers?

One of Claire's neighbors decided to be a taxi driver to help support her family, given inflation sentiments amid rising prices. Rina is a mother of two teenage daughters. She had worked part-time on and off when her kids were younger. But now that they were older and more independent, she thought she would take on a more permanent job that allowed some flexibility in caring for the family and yet earn additional income to pay for the burgeoning household expenses.

She thought of being a taxi driver. Taxi is a popular mode of public transport in Singapore. Fares are generally affordable compared to most cities in developed countries. Taxis charge a flag-down fee, and an additional fee when making a phone booking. There are peak-hour surcharges from 6:00am to 9:30am and from 6:00pm to midnight as these are periods of high demand from people commuting to and from work. There is a midnight peak-hour surcharge from 12:01am to 5:59am where a passenger pays an additional 50% above the meter fare.

Rina could also work for Grab or any of the ride-hailing companies. But she thought that she should start with one of the taxi companies first as she wasn't quite sure how this career move will work out.

Before she applied, Rina scouted around for information on women drivers to assess whether it would be worth her while to consider being a taxi driver. She went online and typed a few keywords – "taxi driver" and "women" – and what popped up was a research paper on the gender wage gap for Singaporean taxi drivers. She thought, "Wow! This hits the nail exactly on the head."

She browsed through the report and while she didn't understand the mumbo jumbo of research talk, Rina thought she got the gist of what the study found. She was excited.

The research by NUS professors studied 554 female taxi drivers over a two-year period. The researchers matched the female drivers with a set of male drivers with similar demographic characteristics including age, marital status, race, religion, educational qualification and driving experience for a fair comparison.

	All	**Men**	**Women**
Hourly earnings (S$)	17.04	17.41	16.53
Working hours in a day	7.61	8.36	6.78
Number of drivers	1106	553	553
Age	50.39	50.22	50.39
Trips per week	82.72	91.41	73.04
Total number of trips	7,186,061	4,181,683	3,004,378

The two-year data set shows that male taxi drivers drive more hours per day (8.36 hours versus 6.78 hours for women) and make more trips (4.2 million versus 3 million for women). Thus, they have higher hourly earnings than female drivers. Moreover, female taxi drivers earn about 4.5% less than male taxi drivers on an hourly basis.

But what Rina found interesting was that female drivers appeared more strategic. Female drivers earn more through bookings than through flag-downs. They accepted more rides that are booked than flag-down rides, indicating a strong preference of female taxi drivers to work through bookings rather than flag-downs. This meant that, while there was a wage gap between male and female taxi drivers, it would have been larger if female drivers relied more on flag-downs than on bookings.

[A] strong preference of female taxi drivers to work through bookings rather than flag-downs.

Then, there was also the matter of when female drivers choose to work. With family commitments in the day and wanting to get the most income when they drive, how do female taxi drivers allocate their driving time?

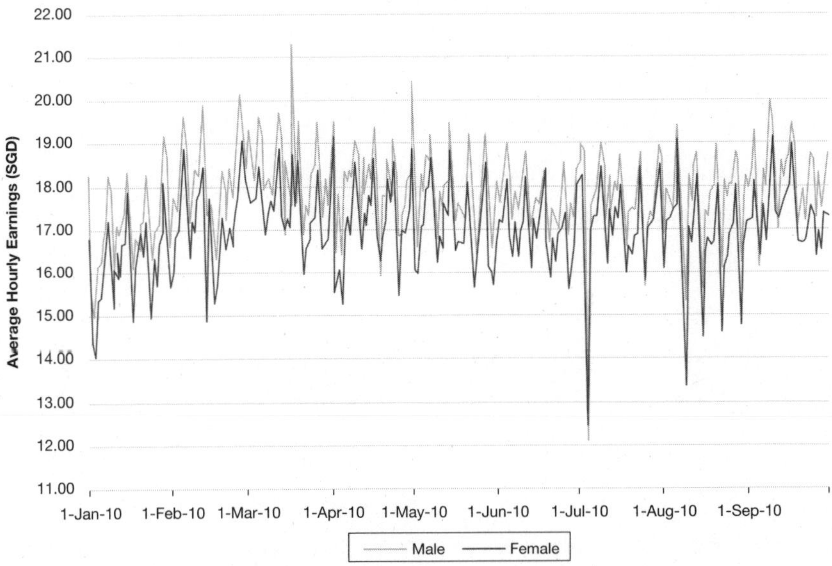

Average Hourly Earnings Between Male and Female Drivers

Typically, drivers have three categories of working hours – peak hours, off-peak hours and midnight hours. There are two segments of peak-hour times – 6:00am to 9:30am, and 6:00pm to 12:00am. There is a surcharge of 25% on top of the metered fares during these hours. The off-peak hours are from 9:30am to 6:00pm, where only the standard metered fare is charged. Midnight hours are from 12:01am to 6:00am, carrying a surcharge of 50% above metered fare. This midnight surcharge allows a taxi driver to earn the highest income per ride.

The demand for taxis is higher during the peak hours of 6:00am to 9:00am and around 3:00pm to 10:00pm. The morning peak hour rides are usually used by people dropping their kids off at school or commuting to work. The evening's peak-hour demand for taxis is largely due to after-work commuting activities. It therefore makes economic sense to work during peak times when there are surcharges.

Rina found that both male and female taxi drivers took more booking rides than flag-down rides during morning peak hours. However, male taxi drivers predominantly fulfilled taxi demand during evening peak hours. Female taxi drivers showed a dip, thus widening the number of evening peak-hour rides between male and female drivers. Female drivers made fewer evening trips than male drivers, despite the evening peak-hour surcharges. However, between flag-downs and bookings, female drivers predominantly worked on bookings during the midnight hours.

"Hmm . . .," thought Rina. "It makes sense to have more bookings than flag-downs because you can make more from booking surcharges. Smart ladies."

Rina read further and learnt that women taxi drivers earned more during the morning peak hours than during the evening peak hours. This was a strategic decision. While male drivers earned more during evening hours to satisfy the evening demand, female drivers earned more by working through bookings during the midnight hours. Despite making fewer total trips, female drivers were able to reduce the wage gap by earning more from midnight bookings than from flag-downs during the same hours. In fact, it may well be that female drivers have developed a repeated clientele base of female passengers who regularly book their rides during the midnight hours. Perhaps these female passengers feel

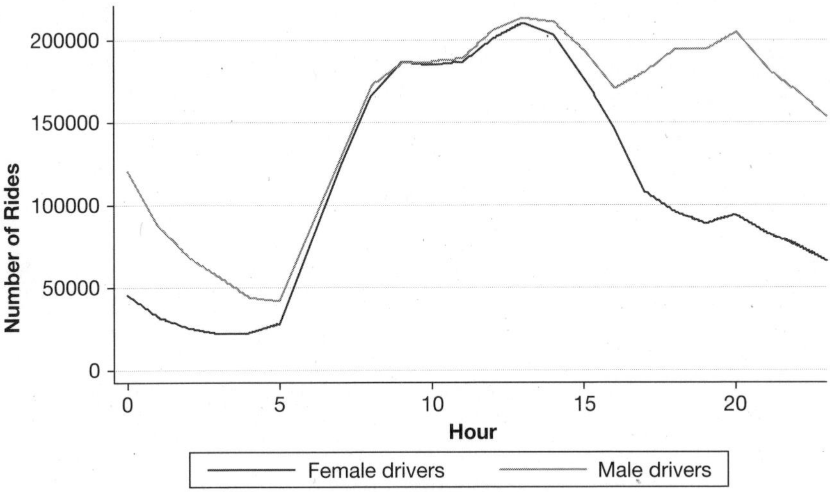

Rides by Flag-down

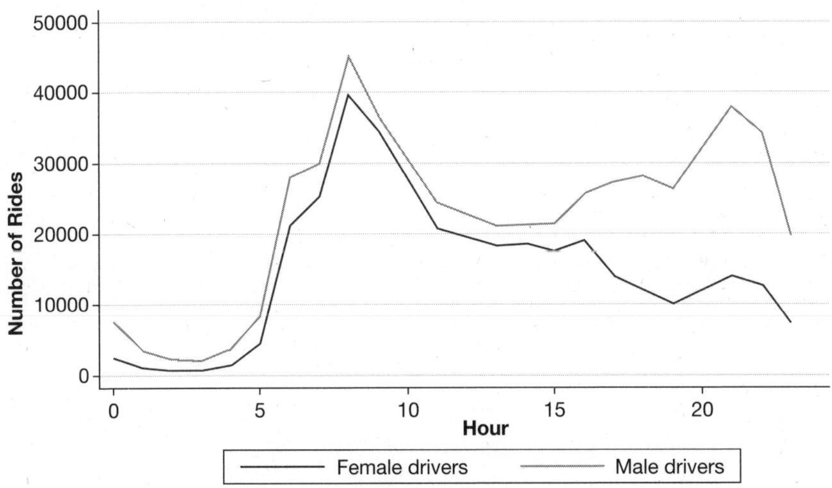

Rides by Booking

safer hiring services of female taxi drivers when they commute at midnight.

"Hmm . . . I should try to get regular female passengers as well, so that I have an assured stream of bookings during the midnight hours," thought Rina to herself.

There were differences between female drivers below and above 50 years old. Those below 50 years old were more likely to adapt their working hour preferences to suit their family responsibilities than older drivers. Younger female drivers preferred to work in the morning when their children were at school, and they chose to attend to their families in the evening despite high peak-hour taxi demand.

In a nutshell, female taxi drivers are strategic. They prefer flexible working hours to maximize their earnings within a self-allocated working time. Although they work fewer hours than their male counterparts, they work strategically during morning peak hours and midnight hours to increase earnings per ride through peak-hour surcharges. They earn more by taking more booking rides than flag-downs during the morning and midnight peak hours. They waste less time driving around to find flag-down passengers. In particular, they rely more on bookings during midnight hours and earn more than male drivers during that time.

"These female drivers are my role models. I will need to have a strategy to ensure that I get the most out of my driving hours," said Rina to herself, smiling as she thought. "Not only should I work hard, I should also work smart."

WANT TO KNOW MORE?

This chapter is based on the following research:

Sumit Agarwal, Shih-Fen Cheng, Tien Foo Sing and Mahanaaz Sultana (2021), "Gender Wage Gap for Singaporean Taxi Drivers: Are Women Strategic Workers?" https://papers.ssrn.com/sol3/papers.cfm?abstract_id=3996148

CHAPTER 12

Like Parent, Like Child; Or Not

"With the rising number of layoffs and inflation, I think more people may become bankrupt if they are highly leveraged and can't pay off their debt," said Cal as she read the online news on bank closures. "Being a bankrupt in Singapore is quite punitive. Singapore's government has very strict regulations."

Indeed. Singapore has one of the strictest debt relief systems worldwide. Unlike countries such as the United States where bankrupt individuals receive a fresh start, declaring bankruptcy in Singapore is very disruptive to a debtor and is usually the last resort for settling debt.

There are three differences between bankruptcy laws in the United States and in Singapore:

1. How a bankruptcy is discharged
2. The number of assets that are exempted
3. The penalties imposed before discharge

Bankrupt individuals in Singapore must repay most of their debt before being discharged from bankruptcy. They are required to make monthly payments under the supervision of a court appointee.

In Singapore, the exempted assets include HDB flats that usually carry a lower market value than private properties. Furniture required for personal use in employment or for family needs, and compulsory savings from CPF (Central Provident Fund) set aside for medical expenses and retirement purposes, are also exempted. Non-exempted assets include private properties and cars. These are sold and the proceeds are put into the bankruptcy estate. The essential purpose is to ensure that the basic needs of bankrupt individuals are met while forcing them to repay their debt as soon as possible.

There are several restrictions on the bankrupt individuals' lifestyle. Their consumption and daily activities are closely monitored. They are not allowed to own cars, private properties or credit cards. They are also prohibited from taking a taxi or having a mobile phone plan. Overseas travel needs the court's approval and only for business purposes. Their career choices are limited as they are not allowed to serve as company directors. There is a loss of privacy as their full name is public information and searchable on the bankruptcy register until they fully repay their debt.

Thus, given the high cost of declaring bankruptcy in Singapore, it is not surprising that the bankruptcy rate is generally low.

"*Heng ah*, bankruptcy rate is low in Singapore," said a relieved Cal. "But still, if you become bankrupt, it would be so difficult not only for the individual but also for the family.

"And not to mention the social penalty. I can well imagine how supposed friends will desert a bankrupt. Moreover, in our Asian society where face-saving is so critical, I wonder whether family members would feel ashamed to be associated with a bankrupt."

"Well, there's some good aspects to that," acknowledged Roy. "If people feel ashamed, they'll steer clear of a lifestyle or decisions that might lead to bankruptcy. And that will break the chain of bankruptcy within the family.

"Or perhaps bankrupt parents can use their tragic situation as a teaching lesson to instill financial prudence in their children.

"In fact, I think they do. I read somewhere about bankrupt individuals and their children. Let me google this online.

"Ah . . . here it is . . ."

Age Effects

A group of NUS professors studied the impact of parental bankruptcy on children's propensity to become bankrupt. They studied the age of children when at least one of their parents declared bankrupt. There were several age groups they were especially interested in – children born after bankruptcy, children aged 0 to 4 years, 5 to 17 years and 18 to 21 years when a parent declared bankrupt.

"Dear, see what the NUS researchers found," said Roy. "They observed that children who experienced parental bankruptcy events at a young age had a significantly lower probability of becoming bankrupt or defaulting on their credit cards."

"That's good news, isn't it?" said Cal.

"I think so. Let's see. Here are more details," Roy added. "Children whose parents were bankrupt before they were born have a bankruptcy risk of 3.4 percentage points lower than that of children who experienced parental bankruptcy at 18 to 21 years of age. A similar finding was observed concerning credit card and other credit facility

[C]hildren who experienced parental bankruptcy events at a young age had a significantly lower probability of becoming bankrupt.

defaults. The default rates of children whose parents were bankrupt before they were born were 3.1 percentage points and 7.6 percentage points lower respectively compared to children who witnessed parental bankruptcy when they were above 18 years old."

"How about children who were around when their parents became bankrupt? Are they more likely to become bankrupts themselves?" enquired Cal.

"Aahh . . .," continued Roy. "The researchers studied them too. For children aged 4 years or younger when their parents became bankrupt, the probability of the children becoming bankrupt in adulthood is 2.7 percentage points lower than that of their older siblings. Their default rates on credit card and other credit facilities were 2 and 5.3 percentage points lower, respectively.

"For those aged 5 to 17 years old when their parents went bankrupt, the probability of bankruptcy is 1.9 percentage points lower, the probability of defaulting on a credit card is 0.9 percentage points lower and the probability of defaulting on other credit facilities is 2.2 percentage points lower than that of those aged 18 years and above."

"How about older children? Would the impact be more severe on them?" asked Cal.

"Wait ah . . .," said Roy as he flipped to the next page of the report. "Aahh . . . here it is. The researchers compared children of bankrupt parents versus those whose parents were not bankrupt. The profs found that for those with parental bankruptcy, children aged 18 and above were 6.8% more likely to declare bankruptcy than those born after bankruptcy. But for children whose parents were not bankrupt, those aged 18 and above were only 2.7% more likely to declare bankruptcy compared to their youngest sibling."

Birth Order Effects

Roy was excited as he thought this research was fascinating. He never knew that there would be intergenerational effects of bankruptcy. He continued reading.

"Dear, the profs found that there may be birth order effects. If firstborn children have to take on more responsibility to support the family because of parental bankruptcy, such added responsibilities may lower their chances of success in adulthood. Firstborn children are more likely to declare bankruptcy and default on credit than non-firstborn children."

"*Aiyoh*," exclaimed Cal. "So poor thing. Firstborn kids have to shoulder more responsibilities that may be detrimental to them through no fault of theirs."

Gender Effects

"I'm biased – I think daughters would be more careful with their money than sons," said Cal with a little smirk.

"Don't be too sure," laughed Roy. "Wait ah . . . let's see whether the profs studied gender effects.

"Oh! They did. They found that daughters whose parents declared bankrupt when they were 5 to 17 years old were 1.5 percentage points less likely to default on credit facilities compared to sons in the same age group.

"For children whose parents were bankrupt when they were 18 to 21 years old, daughters have a 2.3 percentage point lower probability of default on other credit facilities than sons. So, Cal, you are spot on."

Do Children of Bankrupt Parents Undertake More Risks?

The professors studied the risk attitude of such children. Might the age of experiencing the bankruptcy shock of their parents predispose them to take more risks when they grow up? The professors used traffic accidents as a way to measure risk-taking behavior. They found that none of the younger children were more likely to be involved in traffic accidents compared to older children between 18 to 21 years old.

Bankrupt Mothers

"What if the bankrupt parent was the mother? People usually assume the bankrupt parent would be the father. They may be wrong. Would there be more learning opportunities for children if it were the mother who became a bankrupt?" Cal thought aloud.

As a mother, she was keenly aware of how much time she had devoted to teaching her son. Bankrupt parents may devote more time to their children's financial education to ensure that they become more financially prudent. Children may self-learn from their parents' failure and behave more responsibly in their financial decision-making. However, since past research has found mothers to be more effective in shaping the financial behavior of their children, might a bankrupt mother then play a more influential role in her children's financial behavior?

"You know, dear," laughed Roy. "You are asking the same questions as the profs. You may have the makings of a prof!"

"Stop talking rubbish," scolded Cal gently. "Just tell me what the profs found."

Roy didn't want to tease his wife further. "The profs found that if a mother declared bankrupt before her children were born, the probability of her children declaring bankrupt decreases by 3.2 percentage points relative to the probability of children declaring bankrupt when their father declared bankrupt. The probability of defaulting on credit cards or other credit facilities are 8.6 and 13.2 percentage points lower, respectively.

[A] maternal bankruptcy has a stronger positive influence than a paternal bankruptcy.

"For children who experienced a parental bankruptcy at 0 to 4 years old, a maternal bankruptcy reduces the children's probability of declaring bankrupt by 7.1 percentage points relative to that of children who experienced a paternal bankruptcy. Similarly, a maternal bankruptcy has a stronger positive influence than a paternal bankruptcy with the probability of a credit card or other credit facility default decreasing by 2.6 percentage points and 7.4 percentage points, respectively."

"And what if the kids were older? What happened?" asked Cal.

"Hold on. Let me read to you the findings," replied a patient Roy. "It says here that children whose mothers declared bankruptcy when they were 5 to 17 years old were more likely to decrease their risky behavior in adulthood than those whose fathers declared bankruptcy at the same age. A maternal bankruptcy reduces the children's risk for adulthood bankruptcy by 2.4 percentage points, and their risks for defaulting on credit cards or other credit facilities by 0.5 percentage points and 2.2 percentage points, respectively."

"So it looks like our strict bankruptcy laws have a deterrent effect on children of bankrupt parents depending on the age of the children," noted Cal.

"Yes, it looks like it," responded Roy. "It's what the profs call the intergenerational effect. The effects of a strict law are persistent. And in this case, it is good because it seems to deter bankruptcy, more so for selected age groups in the next generation."

With inflation and layoffs, more people may become bankrupt. It can be very difficult on the family.
I wonder how it might affect their children. Do you think their children are more likely to become bankrupt in the future? They may be socialized to bankruptcy being acceptable.
Care
Offer this seat

That may be the case for older children when their parents become bankrupt. But I don't think so for younger kids, especially if they are born after the bankruptcy event.
Hmm . . . Bankrupt parents may have used this situation as a learning lesson to instill in their young children financial prudence. Young kids may also self learn from their parents' mistakes to behave more responsibly. For older kids, it is harder to change for more prudent financial habits.
Care
Offer this seat

A study found that firstborn children are more likely to declare bankruptcy than non-firstborn children.
Among bankrupt parents, daughters are less likely to default than sons.
Show You Care

What if the bankrupt parent is the mother? Do you think there's more impact on the child?
Certainly. Maternal bankruptcy has a stronger influence than paternal bankruptcy, but in a good way.
How so?

Across all ages, a maternal bankruptcy reduces a child's probability of bankruptcy by 3 to 7 percentage points. Mothers are more effective in shaping the financial behavior of their children. They devote more time to their kids' financial education to ensure that they become more financially prudent.

WANT TO KNOW MORE?

This chapter is based on the following research:

Sumit Agarwal, Sing Tien Foo and Xiaoyu Zhang (2022), "Intergenerational Influences on Personal Bankruptcy: Evidence from Singapore," https://papers.ssrn.com/sol3/papers.cfm?abstract_id=4053904

CHAPTER 13

Diet During the Pandemic

"Mum, I want to go out and exercise," grumbled Lizzy. "I can't stand being in the house all the time. As it is, I was already hardly going out before the lockdown. Now with the lockdown, it getting claustrophobic. I need to get out."

"I understand, sweetie," said a sympathetic Claire. "Be patient for a while more, OK? We can discuss how we can arrange for you to go out and yet be safe. We don't want you to get COVID. We don't know what the consequences will be and there's still no remedy yet."

Shortly after the first COVID-19 case was imported into Singapore on 23 January 2020, the number of COVID cases spiked. After employing some mild measures to curb the spread, including the closure of entertainment and worship places, and restriction of crowd density in malls and retail shops, a two-month nationwide lockdown was implemented on 7 April, ending on 1 June. Measures of the lockdown included stay-at-home order, restriction of movement, and closure of schools and most working and eating places. During the lockdown, daily new cases hit a peak at more than 1000 cases and then gradually declined.

"But Mum, it's so frustrating. How to stay in my room all the time? Or walk around in the house only?" pleaded Lizzy.

"I want to meet my friends. I haven't gone to Starbucks for a long time. Or even ate at McDonald's. Or even had a sleepover at Vanessa's place. I'm so tired of eating the same food all the time," Lizzy added.

"Sweetie, we're only two weeks into the lockdown. I am sure the lockdown will end one day. I know it's frustrating. And I'm sorry I don't open a restaurant that offers whatever kind of food you want. But we need to make the best use of what we have," consoled Claire.

"I tell you what. Why don't we order our meals from GrabFood or Deliveroo or FoodPanda on some days? And I'll give you a budget where you can order delivery for snacks. And you can order for your friends too. They can eat in their homes, but you girls can Zoom and eat together online. How's that?"

While that was a solution that Lizzy agreed to, she and many Singaporeans didn't realize that restrictions would still be instituted after the lockdown period was over. Post-lockdown, Singapore gradually reopened in phases. The Safe Reopening phase was from 2 to 18 June, where people could leave home only for essential activities and gradually go back to workplaces and schools. The Safe Transition phase from 19 June to 27 December saw most businesses and schools reopen and small gatherings of up to five persons were allowed.

Eating in restaurants or even food courts and hawker centers were still not allowed and ordering in became part of what almost all Singaporeans do on a regular basis.

"What did you order for lunch this time, Lizzy?" asked Claire one day.

"Barbecued pork and fried gyoza," was Lizzy's fast reply.

"No vegetables?" asked Claire.

"Don't like veg, Mum," said a bored Lizzy, tapping her feet as she listened to BTS' *Dynamite*. Typical of many teenagers, she didn't like her mother asking too many questions.

"Didn't you order fried chicken wings yesterday? And sticks of fried sotong for snacks with your friends?" enquired Claire.

She felt that Lizzy had been ordering unhealthy barbecued and fried foodstuff way too often, much to her dislike. She had read online that Singaporeans' eating habits had changed during the lockdown.

Based on a study of an online platform that offers take-away and food delivery services with data on food ordering, the research found that there was a declining trend of vegetable orders after the lockdown began. This decline persisted after the lockdown ended. The probability that an order would include vegetables declined by 20% to 30%.

[T]he probability of Singaporeans ordering unhealthy food went up by 10% to 20% since the lockdown started and persisted even after the lockdown was lifted.

On the other hand, the probability of Singaporeans ordering unhealthy food went up by 10% to 20% since the lockdown started and persisted even after the lockdown was lifted. The probability of Singaporeans ordering beverages went up by 3.9%.

The above trends were observed for Singaporeans living in HDB flats as well as private residences.

What about the time when a food delivery order was placed? Because of the mandatory stay-at-home order during the lockdown, food delivery service users like Lizzy may delay their meals to a later time in the day, like midnight. The study also found that for non-midnight orders, the probability of vegetable ordering dropped by 15%, while the probability of ordering unhealthy food and beverages increased by 11% and 4%, respectively.

You ordered food delivery again?
Yah, mum. Barbecued pork and fried gyoza.
No veg?
Nope.

You've been ordering a lot of unhealthy food and not enough vegetables during the lockdown. That's not good.
It seems like the more COVID cases there are, the more you order unhealthy food and less veg.

Professor Sumit:
With the lockdown, orders of unhealthy food increased by 10 to 20% and persisted even after the lockdown was lifted.
The probability that an order will include vegetables went down by 20 to 30%.
For every 1% increase in the number of COVID cases, the next day saw a 0.02% increase in unhealthy food ordering, and 0.04% decrease in vegetable ordering.

The researchers also studied the number of COVID cases for each day to see whether the number of cases would affect food delivery orders for the day after. It turned out that the number of disclosed COVID cases was linked with unhealthier eating habits. In particular, the researchers found that for every 1% increase in the number of cases the day before, it resulted in a 0.04% decrease in vegetable ordering probability, a 0.02% increase in unhealthy food ordering probability, and a 0.01% increase in beverage ordering probability. All these impacts were significant.

Claire shook her head as she read the online news.

"This isn't good for our bodies," she said to herself. "Not only are we eating less healthily, I don't think we are exercising as much either, since we are stuck at home. I had better watch what Lizzy orders. She's not going to like it."

WANT TO KNOW MORE?

This chapter is based on the following research:

Sumit Agarwal, Peiying Huang, Chenxi Luo, Yu Qin and Changwei Zhan (2021), "Assessment of Online Food Ordering and Delivery in Singapore During the COVID-19 Pandemic," *JAMA Network Open*, Vol. 4, No. 9, ie 2126466 doi: 10:1001/jamanetworkopen.2021.26466

CHAPTER 14

En Bloc Sales

Roy and Cal are still contemplating upgrading to a condo. Although they had initially wanted a fairly new condo for that "feel good" sentiment when living there, prices have been getting more and more out of their reach.

The other possibility is to buy an old property. For sure, some renovations will be needed and maintenance may be higher. Older properties tend to be dilapidated with outdated structures. But the built-in size tends to be bigger in older properties than newer ones. And there may be the possibility of an en bloc.

En bloc or collective sale is the process in which private developers acquire multi-family developments from all individual property owners collectively, demolish the existing structure, and build brand new residential developments on the land.

En bloc sales are appealing to developers because unlike Government Land Sales where the government releases state land for sale with lease

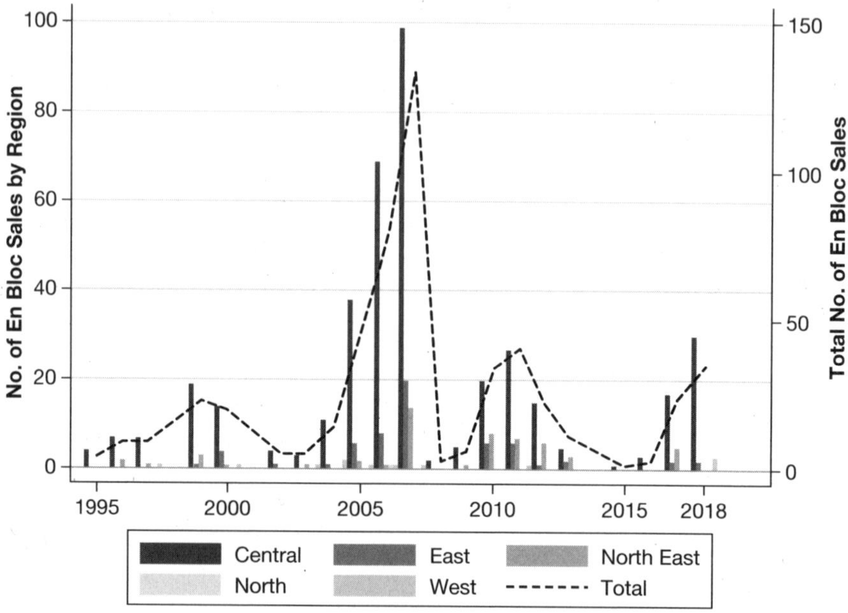

Distribution of En Bloc Activities by Year and Region

terms of 99 years, en bloc sales give developers an opportunity to acquire freehold residential land. Freehold land is highly sought after in land-scarce Singapore.

"Cal, let's explore some old condos. If we are lucky, we might be able to strike an en bloc jackpot a few years after living there," said Roy. "Then, we can buy a bigger and newer condo."

The idea of a windfall is appealing. Roy has heard stories of people who were living in rundown private apartments with escalating maintenance fees. Prices of these apartments were low as few buyers wanted to live in a beat-up place. But when developers offered to buy over the estate, owners of these properties enjoyed a big windfall. And so the craze for en bloc sales began. However, Roy has heard of dilapidated properties that were unsuccessful en bloc attempts. Some homeowners were too greedy and held out for astronomical prices that developers were not interested in.

"What kind of condo should we look at?" asked Cal.

"I think en bloc opportunities are higher for properties that are old and have fewer units. The consent of at least 80% of owners in the estate is needed before en bloc negotiations can take place," replied Roy.

"I remember there was a newspaper report mentioning that the average age of en bloc buildings is about 26 years old. Properties aged 20 to 29 years made up the largest share of 47% of the total en bloc sales, followed by properties aged 30 years above which constituted 31%.

"Since we intend to stay there for a few years first, and those that are really old would have their en bloc potential factored in the asking price, I think we should look at those about 15 years old whose asking price is hopefully not as high as those more than 20 years old. These would be the next set of private properties to go en bloc in the future.

"And we should look at estates with fewer units. Apparently, the average number of units in en bloc properties is 47 units, which is about three times smaller than that in non-en bloc projects. Smaller projects are more likely to be sold en bloc because there are fewer owners that will resist and hold up the negotiation process."

Cal nodded in agreement. Roy continued.

"Such low-density projects have lower demolition costs which developers like, as it saves them money.

"Also, developers like properties with a low built-up density as this increases the redevelopment potential. I remember reading somewhere that an en bloc probability increases by 2.4 percentage points for every 1 unit of permissible gross plot ratio."

"Hmm . . . what about being near MRT stations? Would that increase en bloc potential?" asked Cal as she took note of the property characteristics to look for.

"Near MRT stations would be fantastic. But there are very limited private freehold properties near MRT stations. So, I think the next best set of potential en bloc properties would be those near primary schools," said Roy.

Cal understood the rationale. Priority of a place in Primary 1 registration is given to residents living within 1- and 2-kilometer radius of a school. Properties within this radius are therefore popular, especially if a primary school has a high academic reputation.

A few days later, Cal updated Roy on her research into various old condos that were advertised for sale. She had seen a couple of ads about walkup apartments in the Orchard Road area. There were a few units in a very old private estate at Cavenagh Road. These properties were within walking distance of Somerset MRT station and various shopping centers along Orchard Road.

Roy had done his own research. He had called one of his friends who worked in one of the bigger property firms.

"Eh, John. I may be buying an old apartment with the possibility of an en bloc sale a few years down the road. How's the en bloc market like?" Roy asked John.

"The en bloc market is good. After all, how else is a developer going to get freehold property, *siah*?" replied John.

"Freehold properties are scarce in Singapore. If you have one, you are sitting on a gold mine. But it's not easy to find old properties at low prices now. These owners have gotten smart and have jacked up their prices for people like you who want to buy property in anticipation of a future en bloc sale."

"Hey! But I may be lucky, *leh*. Cal and I will use our charm to sweet talk an owner into selling his place to us at a fair price," chuckled Roy.

"If you do, then you are lucky," said John. "On average, these properties with redevelopment potential sell at a premium of 20% to 29%. So, owners have already factored the en bloc potential in their asking price."

"Hmm . . . so there are anticipative effects?" moaned Roy.

[P]roperties with redevelopment potential sell at a premium of 20% to 29%.

"Of course," came John's reply. "These owners are not dumb. Their properties may be old, but money is still money. We find that resale prices of en bloc properties increase at an average rate of 0.03% and 0.05% per month as transactions draw closer to the successful en bloc event date.

"Compared to how resale transactions occurred more than a year before a property is en bloc-ed, there is a price premium of about 14% if the property is sold within 6 months of the en bloc event, and about 8% in 6 to 12 months to the en bloc event.

"The more certainty of a property going en bloc, the higher will be the resale price. So, my advice would be to look for an old property where talk of an en bloc is remote. This way, you can get it at a lower price. But then, there is greater uncertainty of an en bloc. So, it has to be a property that you are prepared to live in if the en bloc is unsuccessful."

WANT TO KNOW MORE?

This chapter is based on the following research:

Liu Ee Chia and Tien Foo Sing (2023), "Redevelopment Values in Multi-Family Properties: Evidence from En Bloc Sales in Singapore," *Journal of Housing Economics*, Vol. 60, https://www.sciencedirect.com/science/article/abs/pii/S1051137723000190

CHAPTER 15

HDB Upgrading

"*Aiyoh*! If sellers already factored in the en bloc potential in their asking price, then I'm not sure we want to take the risk of paying a premium and realize later that there will be no en bloc after all," said Cal, after hearing what John, Roy's property developer friend, had to say about en bloc price premium.

"Perhaps we should look for older HDB flats that may be slated for upgrading. The upgrading may add value to the price."

More than 80% of Singapore's population live in HDB flats. Started in the early 1960s to provide housing for the population, HDB has improved the quality with larger and better designed flats in the 1970s. The improvement in the quality of new flats has continued since.

One way in which older HDB flats are improved on is a series of subsidized upgrading programs undertaken by the government. There is the Main Upgrading Programme which involves renovation of the flat, the block and the precinct. There is a space-adding item (SAI) that flat owners can vote on whether to undertake or not. This involves building an additional 6 square meters of space that can be used as a storeroom or a small bedroom. Regardless of the original size of the flat, the same amount of space is added if flat owners vote to have it.

Despite subsidies from the government, some flat owners voted against SAI. Firstly, SAI would be inconvenient as the construction of SAI would be carried out right next to existing units. Secondly, flat owners have to pay quite a substantial amount if they opt for SAI. For example, 1- to 3-room flat owners have to pay about $9000 after subsidy if they opt for SAI. Thirdly, some flat owners simply do not need additional space.

Whether they buy a private property or another public property, Cal wants to ensure that they make the right decision given the hefty property prices.

"Roy, did you ask John about upgraded HDB flats?" asked Cal.

"Yah, I did," replied Roy. "John told me that such SAI increases the resale price of a flat by an average of 7%. However, the degree of price appreciation varies."

"Varies?" asked a curious Cal. "Based on what?"

[S]maller flats experienced substantial price increase.

"Size of flat," was Roy's response. "John said that not everyone saw their flat price appreciate to the same extent when they added more space as part of the upgrading program. It seems that smaller flats experienced substantial price increase, while the larger flats maintained roughly the same price level."

"Huh? Got like that one *meh*?" said Cal, breaking out in Singlish whenever she's excited.

"Yah. Flats that were originally less than 55 square meters experienced a 16% increase or about $26,500 increase, after accounting for the added space. Those between 55 and 65 square meters experienced a 9% increase or about $15,500.

"Those more than 75 square meters actually experienced falls in their unit price by 8% to 9% after SAI. But because of the increase in housing space by 6 square meters, the total value of the flat remained roughly the same."

"So the additional space is still worth it *lah*?" continued Cal.

"Yup, I guess so. Even for larger units, the added space helped it to retain its price," Roy nodded.

Such upgrading appears to be a good investment in general, especially for smaller units.

WANT TO KNOW MORE?

This chapter is based on the following research:

Sumit Agarwal, Yanying Chen, Jing Li, and Yi Jin Tan (2019), "Hedonic Price of Housing Space," *Real Estate Economics*, Vol. 49(2), pp. 574-609, https://onlinelibrary.wiley.com/doi/abs/10.1111/1540-6229.12298

Roy, do you think it's worth buying flats that will be upgraded with space-adding feature? Each flat gets an additional 6m2 of space that can be used as a store room or a small bedroom.
I heard such upgrading increases resale price by 7%
1
2
3
4

Is this for all sizes?
The smaller flats benefit the most. They rose by 16%. But for bigger flats, the unit price actually declined. But because of the added space, the total value of the flat remained almost the same.

CHAPTER

16 Online Listings

"Dear, there are so many property listings online now. It's so convenient to look for something you like, screen the properties first, then contact the agent for a property visit," Cal told Roy as she scrolled PropertyGuru, an online property website, to assess how much their HDB flat could sell for.

"I wonder how people had the patience to go through ads in the newspapers. I remember when my parents were looking for a place to buy, they would read the Classified Ads in *The Straits Times*, circle those they were interested in, call the agent and arrange for a visit. It was so time consuming. The online listing is a lot more efficient and convenient."

"Oh! More than that, the online portal also benefits property agents," said Roy.

"How so?" asked Cal. She knows Roy has a good friend working in the property development industry and they had gone golfing over the weekend. The friend must have updated Roy on recent developments in the property market.

"Ah . . . you know *lah*. The government has been encouraging Singapore to be a smart nation. So we have fintech, right? Many businesses have QR codes for people to scan and make payments. We also have PayLah and PayNow for virtual payments. And then there are various wallet pay apps on phones.

"Likewise, there's proptech for the property industry. The online portal is a proptech tool to make the industry more advanced and efficient to benefit everyone – both a property seller and a property buyer, as well as a property agent.

"Proptech improves information transparency and enables buyers to search more efficiently for properties of their choice. Of course, it does not guarantee that every listing will eventually lead to a successful sale.

"John told me how the use of online portals benefitted sellers and property agents. He said that agents sell houses at an average premium of 3.3% by adopting online listings instead of advertising on Classified Ads in newspapers. So assuming that there are slightly over 40,000 transactions sold via online portals at an average of $1.3 million. This works out to about $1.7 billion of economic value added to listing properties online.

"As agents typically charge a brokerage fee of 1%, this would translate to an increase in brokerage fees of $17.1 million! A whopping sum!"

"There are so many listings online. I know it's more convenient, but there're so many listings that I feel I can be easily overwhelmed," said Cal.

"True. As to be expected, the more listings there are, the more competition there is, and chances of successful online listing decline. Even if a real estate agent could secure exclusive listing rights from potential sellers, he would still find it challenging to sell an apartment in a project with few transactions compared to one in a more popular project with many past transactions. The exclusive listing does not guarantee a successful sale," Roy explained.

"John told me that larger condo units with freehold tenure have favorable characteristics that increase the probability of a sale in proptech markets."

"What are these characteristics?" asked an impatient Cal. She thought her husband could be quite long-winded at times.

"Well, being close to the city center decreases the probability of a successful transaction," replied Roy quickly.

"Huh? Really? I thought being close to the city is an asset," said a surprised Cal.

"While that may be true, think about who buys such properties. These properties tend to be more expensive and attract more interest from foreign buyers. But it is the average local buyers who are more likely to use online channels, not foreign buyers. Moreover, local buyers usually search for properties further from the city center. So there is somewhat of a mismatch.

"On the other hand, being close to an MRT station increases the probability of a successful transaction, and properties near MRT stations are highly popular and easier to sell online.

"According to John, how effective these online listings are to agents depends on three factors:

1. How well an agent can harness online portals to expand their listing activities and reach out to a larger pool of potential buyers.
2. The writing style – is how readable the listing is.
3. The type of portal used."

"So what did he find?" Cal prodded.

"He said that agents with more online listings devote more effort and have a higher probability of selling these listed properties than agents who are less active.

"But those with too many simultaneous listings, by project or by property at any given time, are unable to focus and do not act as effectively in converting their listings into sales. Their effort became diluted. They get distracted by the volume of requests from both sellers and potential buyers."

"I'm intrigued by 'the writing style'. What about it?" asked Cal.

"Ahh . . . this is about how readable the listing is. Is the text easy to understand?" continued Roy.

"John said that buyers are not influenced by overly hyped wording in a listing. Words such as 'lovingly', 'masterfully', 'brisk' and 'methodical' are high on sentiments. Descriptions with high sentiments give the impression of exaggeration, which reduces chances of a potential buyer pursuing the property."

[B]uyers are not influenced by overly hyped wording in a listing.

"I guess using such descriptions may raise some credibility issues among potential buyers. While for others, expectations may have been raised, and they go away disappointed when the property doesn't quite match their expectations based on the listing description," said Cal.

"That may well be the case," responded Roy. "John said that if more words are used in a listing to clarify what the property is, it helps to increase the chances of a successful sale. But the description doesn't need to have lots of numbers.

"Then there is the issue of whether to post a listing on multiple portals, and whether to list on popular portals. John says that agents who use multiple portals have a higher chance of selling a property than those with a single portal. I think that's quite understandable.

"However, using a popular portal appears not to be an advantage. Popular portals are overcrowded with many listed properties and so agents can receive overwhelming attention from non-serious potential buyers. Instead, using smaller niche-market-oriented portals is beneficial in closing sales because it is more focused and has less competition.

"In John's opinion, what's interesting is that, while agents can sell their properties relatively faster, there is a disadvantage to sellers. Because of the more intense competition in a popular portal, there is a likelihood that real estate agents who list there compete on time at the expense of price premiums."

"Maybe these agents are willing to reduce the price for a quick sale because they do not have exclusive marketing rights and so are not motivated to sell the property at a higher price," observed Cal.

"You may be right, dear. We always hear of agents who'd rather have a bird in hand than two in the bush. They want to get a quick commission and move on to the next property. They are looking out more for their own interest than interest of the seller," said Roy.

"Yeah. I remember a colleague who told me that her agent kept harassing her to sell her investment property just before an upswing in property prices. She's still so upset that the agent put pressure on her to let go. Even though the agent made a smaller commission at the lower price, he had other properties to sell and he knew my friend was an easy target for a quick sale," Cal described, shaking her head.

"But what if agents use both multiple and popular portals? What happens?" she asked Roy.

"Well, I guess the effects offset each other. Using the most popular portal reduces the price difference between the listing price and the transacted price. But the properties sell faster. The intense competition in a popular portal may push real estate agents who list there to compete on time at the expense of price premiums."

"Why might that be the case? It is afterall a popular portal," asked Cal.

"I think the downward pressure on prices in the popular portal could be due to real estate agents not given exclusive marketing rights. Hence, they have no incentive to sell properties at higher prices," replied Roy.

He continued, "But using multiple portals helps in increasing the transacted price above the listed price. However, it takes a longer time to sell a property. So, agents who use multiple portals as well as the popular portal end up selling a property at a price close to the listing price, but not as close as if they had only listed on a popular portal. In terms of the number of days a property is listed before it is sold, it would be longer but not as long as when a listing was on multiple portals only."

WANT TO KNOW MORE?

This chapter is based on the following research:

Tien Foo Sing and Yiheng Zou (2021), "Improving Information Efficiency in Housing Markets Using Online Listings," https://papers.ssrn.com/sol3/papers.cfm?abstract_id=3772412

17

CHAPTER

Fintech

"We talked so much about proptech. How about fintech? After all, Singapore is a financial hub. I don't know how true this is – I heard that when some big banks closed down in Europe, funds flowed into Singapore because we were a safe haven," said Cal.

"Oh . . . we have made much progress in fintech. Take mobile payment for instance," replied Roy.

"Mobile payment offers advantages over cash payment by reducing costs and alleviating friction in transactions. By removing the need to carry cash, mobile payment improves convenience for consumers.

"For merchants, especially those who are more reliant on cash, they also benefit from the reduction in cash-handling costs. There is less cash leakage as employee theft is minimized. How to steal cash when there is no cash transaction, right?

"Here . . . this is a report that shows some of the effects of fintech on Singapore businesses," said Roy, as he rummaged his drawer and handed an article to Cal.

QR-code Payment

The article reported on a study which showed that the cost reduction benefits of mobile payment technology had a profound impact on the economy. When frictions in business operations are eased, business growth is encouraged, especially for new businesses that would otherwise be deterred due to the high cost of handling cash.

From a consumer's perspective, the convenience of mobile payment facilitates more adoption of the technology. Mobile payment reduces the transaction costs to both consumers and merchants, which in turn increases consumers' spending capacity and spurs their demand for more products and services, leading to more businesses adopting mobile payment to increase sales.

As of 2018, the rate of mobile payment in the United States stands at 20%. In China, where mobile payment is the norm, the annual growth rate of mobile payment transactions was 96% from 2013 to 2018.

Singapore has a well-developed infrastructure for mobile payment. As part of the Smart Nation Vision, the Quick Response (QR) code payment tool was introduced in April 2017. This mobile payment technology allows consumers to make transactions or transfer funds by displaying or scanning QR codes on their mobile phones. The QR-code payment tool is straightforward, efficient and secure, which reduces transaction costs, particularly for small and new businesses. Additionally, unlike cashless payment technologies such as credit cards, which charge 2% to 3% transaction fees, there is no transaction costs to consumers and businesses for mobile payment.

"I remember when the QR code was introduced," remarked Cal. "It was convenient to use, though initially, I was a bit hesitant because of security

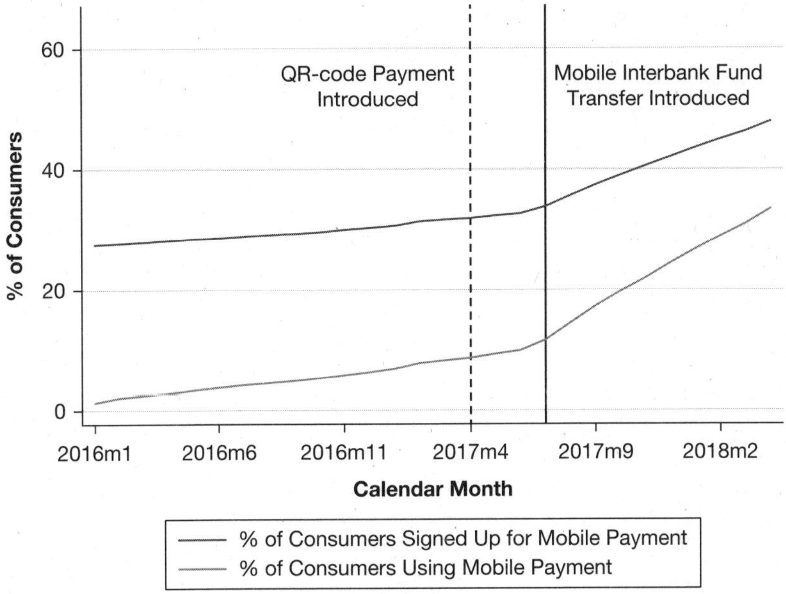

Number of Consumers Who Use or Sign up for Mobile Payment

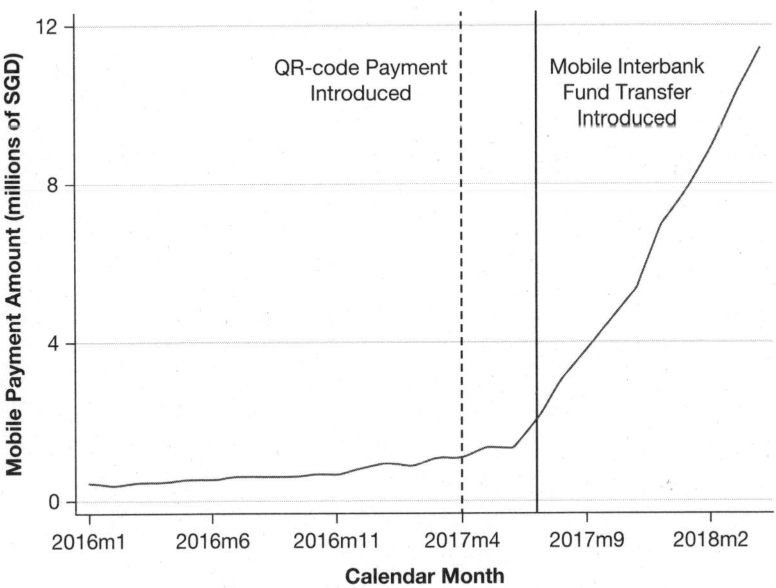

Total Dollar of Mobile Payment Transactions

concerns. But I think almost everyone uses it now. How was the take up rate then?"

Roy responded. "About a year after the QR-code payment tool was introduced, there was a surge in mobile payment adoption. Consumers who used or signed up for mobile payment went up from 32% to 48%, equivalent to a 43% increase. So, I would think the adoption of QR code is quite successful.

"Not only that, it seems that people spend more using the QR code. The report says that the total dollar amount of mobile payment transactions exhibited a significantly large increase, by almost 10 times. This implies that mobile payment adopters became more active after the technology was introduced."

"We also have PayNow," said Cal. "Did the study include PayNow? That's another fintech tool. I think it was introduced in July, three months after QR code was made available."

"Hmm . . .," said Roy as he studied the report. "It says here that there was evidence that mobile payment adoption was further accelerated. This means that the introduction of another fintech tool such as PayNow reinforced the impact of QR-code payment and further promoted mobile payment usage."

New Business Creation

Roy continued. "The report also talked about business creation. Prior to the introduction of mobile payment technology in Singapore, business creation for both consumer and industrial products were similar. However, since such technology benefits consumers immensely by offering convenience, the impact on consumer business was more pronounced."

"How so?" asked Cal. She has a few friends who have started their own businesses and may be interested in the value of fintech to their businesses.

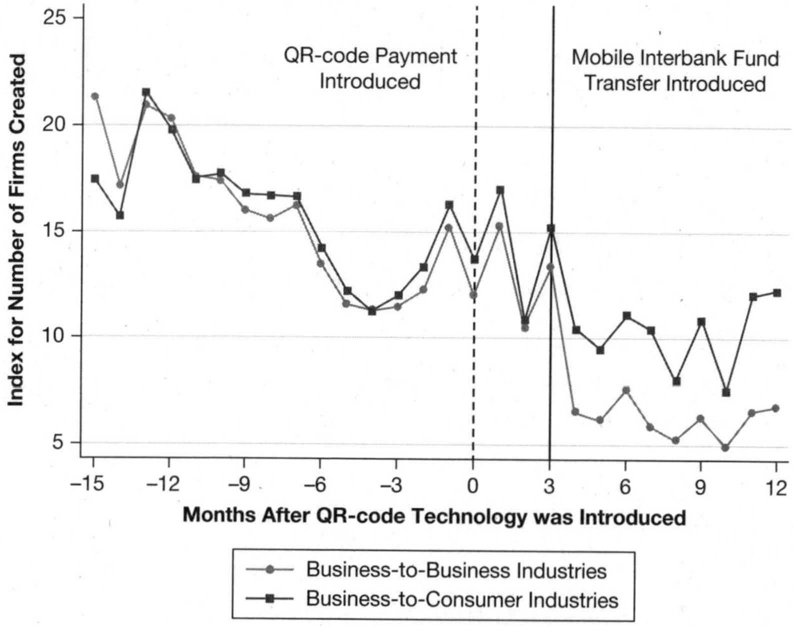

Number of New Businesses Created

"It seems that business creation among business-to-consumer (B2C) industries increased by 9% per month compared to business-to-business industries," replied Roy. "On average, there were about 1500 firms created each month in B2C industries prior to April 2017. After fintech was introduced in April 2017, the number of such new firms rose by 132 per month."

It seems that business creation among business-to-consumer (B2C) industries increased.

Small Business Creation

"Roy, does the report say whether small businesses benefitted from fintech?" asked Cal.

"Yep. It seems small businesses benefitted. The researchers said that the benefit of mobile-payment technology was more pronounced for small businesses. These businesses include sole proprietorships that rely extensively on cash payment. Hence, the use of a more convenient payment method facilitated more consumer purchases from such businesses.

"I think this is important because small businesses is a vital component of the economy and is a key engine of economic growth. So I'm glad to hear that small businesses benefitted from fintech."

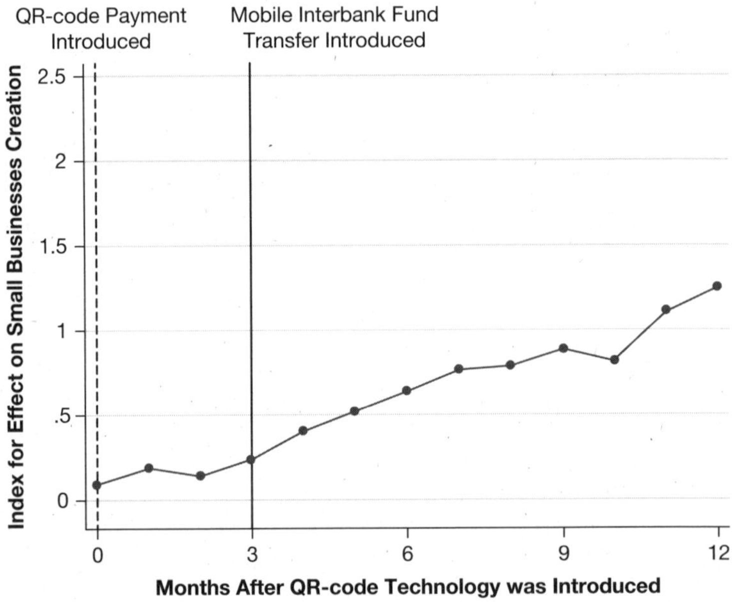

Effect of Mobile-Payment Technology on Small Business Creation

Industries with High vs Low Cash-handling Costs

Although small businesses generally profited from mobile-payment technology, such businesses vary in the costs incurred to handle cash transactions. For instance, grocery stores and petrol stations have relatively higher costs of handling cash than businesses in the retail trade and food businesses.

The number of small business creation in high-cash-handling-cost industries increased by 44% per month, while there was no clear increase in low-cash-handling-cost industries such as retail and food industries.

More vs Less Wealthy Neighborhoods

Residential house prices was used as a proxy for the average wealth of a neighborhood. In low house price areas, the introduction of mobile-payment technology increased small business creation by 13% per month compared to 6% in high house price areas.

Similarly, small businesses in HDB areas benefitted more from this fintech tool than non-HDB areas.

Tourism vs Non-tourism Areas

Tourism is a major part of the Singapore economy. In tourist areas, merchants serve a higher proportion of tourists who do not have access to the mobile-payment technology that is oriented toward local use. Therefore, such fintech benefitted businesses outside tourism areas more as they were targeted at locals.

Consumer's Cash Usage

"How about the amount of cash we carry? I would think that, with fintech, people will carry less cash," said Cal. "In fact, I noticed that more and more of my young colleagues only carry their phone, while some also carry a card holder. They don't carry cash anymore."

"This will vary depending on age group, isn't it?" responded Roy. "Singaporeans differ in how much cash they use. Older Singaporeans feel more comfortable using cash, especially for small transactions. They will still carry cash. Those who are more tech savvy with access to mobile phones are more likely to use mobile-payment technology than their less tech savvy peers."

Cal, do you know that QR codes and PayNow have accelerated mobile payment usage? A year after QR code was introduced in Singapore, mobile payment adoption went up by 43%
面包店和糖果店
BAKERY & CONFECTIONARY
Ice Cold
NEWSPAPER
I think businesses must have flourished from more consumers willing to spend.
Yah. More new businesses were created especially in the business-to-consumer industries.
Ice Cold
Small businesses that rely a lot on cash payment benefitted. Mobile payments facilitated more purchases.
You mean like grocery stores and petrol stations where there is high cost in handling cash?
Exactly. The number of small businesses in high-cost-handling industries went up by 44% per month.

And did you notice that there are now more new businesses in our HDB neighborhood? Well, mobile-payment technology has increased creation of such businesses in HDB areas by 13%
BUBBLE
TEA
H

But does it mean that as consumers, we spend more?
Well, we found that consumers increased their mobile payment amount by $2.50 a month. If you project that to the population, that amounts to a sizeable $4.5 million.
Cut

"I'm sure those with prior experience of mobile payment would use less cash," commented Cal.

"You are right," responded Roy. "Singaporeans who have previous experience of mobile payment usage are more receptive to fintech payment technology than those with little or no such experience. In fact, according to the report, tech savvy consumers increased their mobile payment amount by $2.50 per month which, when projected to the population, amounts to $4.5 million."

ATM Closure

"I bet there are fewer ATMs now, since more and more Singaporeans aren't carrying cash," said Cal.

"Right on, dear," said Roy. "With increasing use of mobile payment and less use of cash, it is not surprising to find that ATMs are closing down at an increasing rate after the introduction of this technology. The number of ATM closures increased from an average of 12 per month before April 2017 to 17 per month after.

"More importantly, the rate of ATM closures is associated with small business creation. Areas where there is high growth of small business creation saw a higher acceleration of ATM closures."

Credit Card Usage

Cal thought through more about the consequences of using mobile payment. "While it is understandable that the use of mobile payments will substitute the use of cash, does it also cannibalize credit card usage?" she thought to herself.

In fact, the article reported that credit card spending increased with mobile payment usage. Singaporeans appear to enjoy the liquidity provided by credit cards as well as the promotional benefits.

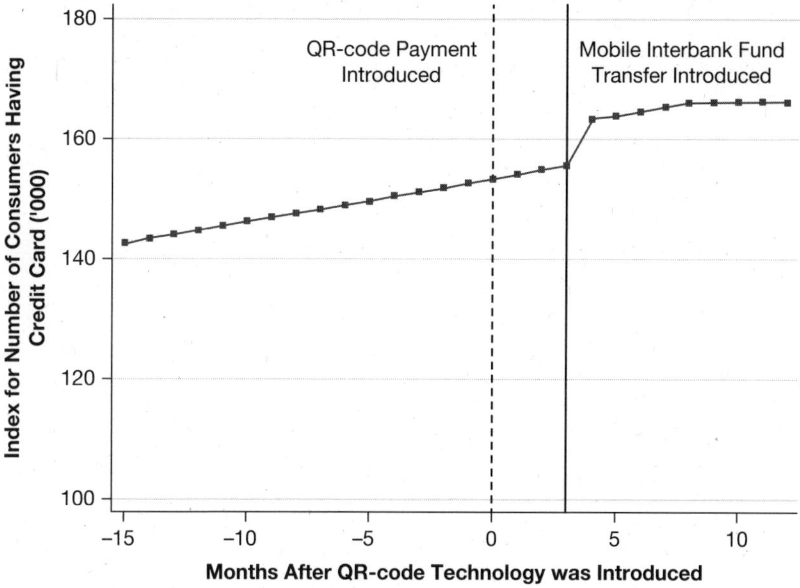

Number of Consumers Having a Credit Card

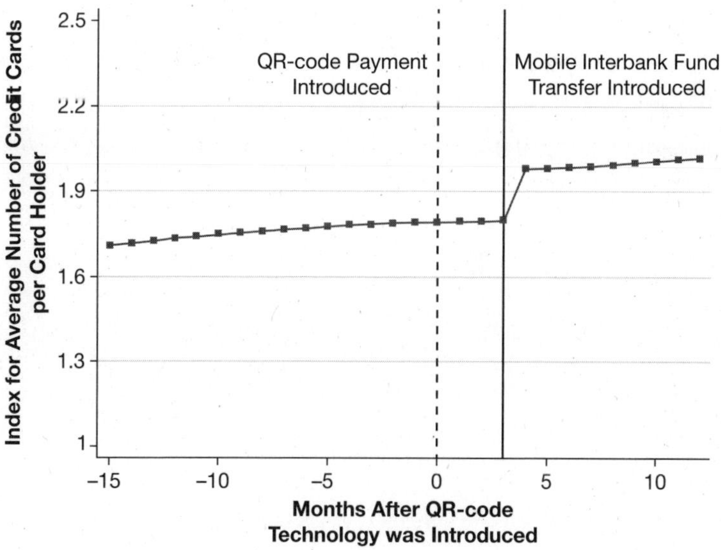

Average Number of Credit Cards Held by a Card Holder

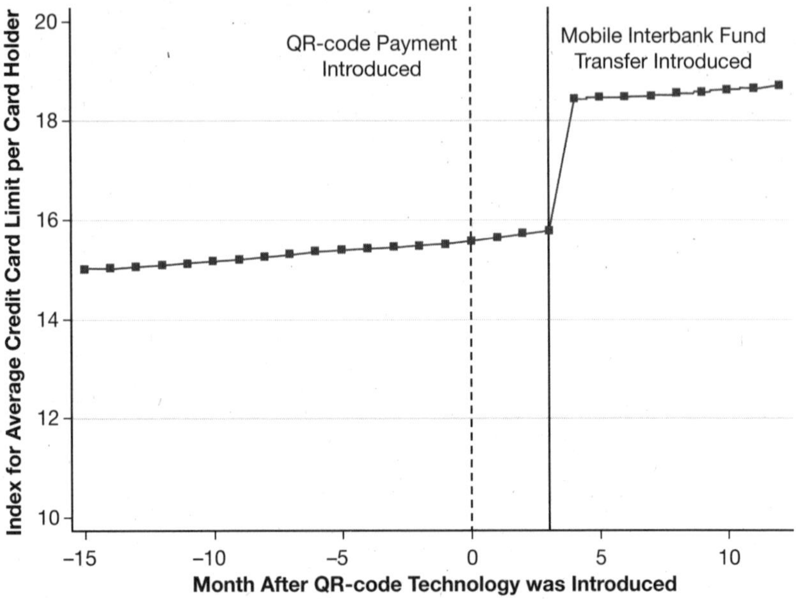

Average Credit Card Limit per Card Holder

Banks may also have something to do with the increase in credit card usage. Given the high profit margin of credit cards, banks are incentivized to maintain their market share of this business. They may have increased credit provision in response to mobile payment technology. Indeed, Singaporeans with experience of mobile payment usage exhibited a 1.6% increase in probability of becoming a credit card holder when mobile payment technology was introduced.

Moreover, the total number of consumers with credit cards and the average number of credit cards as well as credit limit per cardholder saw significant increases after mobile payment technology came about.

WANT TO KNOW MORE?

This chapter is based on the following research:

Sumit Agarwal, Wenlan Qian, Yuan Ren, Hsin-Tien Tsai and Bernard Yeung (2020), "The Real Impact of FinTech: Evidence from Mobile Payment Technology," https://papers.ssrn.com/sol3/papers.cfm?abstract_id=3556340

CHAPTER 18

Cybersecurity Breaches

"Hey! Now that so many people have so much confidential info on their mobile phones, I'm worried that there will be more security breaches," said a concerned Cal.

"Or, for that matter, security breaches on any online platform. I shop on Lazada, Shopee and Amazon. I use Grab for transport and food delivery. And not to mention the occasional merchants I buy from directly online. They have my credit card details.

"Can you imagine what will happen if I lose my phone? My bank accounts are in there, my credit cards, PayNow, PayLah, Apple Pay, and all my emails. Scary *leh*. I'll be so vulnerable.

"If I lose my phone in Singapore, it's already troublesome enough. But I'll feel less frantic because I can easily go to the nearest computer and lock my phone down. It's also easier for me to cancel my cards when I'm in Singapore. But can you imagine if this happened when I'm overseas? I'll be so so worried."

"I know. Scary, right?" nodded Roy. "So, all the more reason why we should be careful. And maybe travel in a group so we can look out for each other and help should such an incident occur.

"For online sites, these companies must harness their security system and be a step ahead of cyber criminals. Every piece of internet activity such as search, click and transaction, generates some data. Since the majority of the world's population are online users, can you imagine the explosive growth in digital data?"

"What about food delivery and ride-sharing platforms? We order a lot online, dear," Cal reminded him. "I would think these sites have a lot of personal data."

"Definitely. Food delivery and ride-sharing platforms offer digital services that store and harvest private and even confidential consumer data," nodded Roy. "If there is a cybersecurity breach, it can lead to large scale data leakages and pose substantial privacy concern for users of these digital services. Did you know that, in 2021, there were 178 incidents of data breaches just in the public sector alone?

"Globally, there were data breaches incurred by Yahoo! and eBay involving 3 billion and 143 million accounts, respectively. In Singapore, Eatigo was fined for data breach that resulted in the sale of 2.8 million users' personal data. Even RedMart had a data breach when names, email addresses and other personal data of about 900,000 users were stolen from its database and put up for sale online. Many companies have had cybersecurity breaches, including Carousell, Starbucks and even cosmetics company Clarins.

"You know what? Let me check with my friend, Sumit. He's a professor who's done research in the United States, China, India and Singapore. Let's see whether he knows what happens when there is a cybersecurity breach."

Roy texted Sumit.

"Hey, Sumit! My wife is concerned about cybersecurity breaches," related Roy. "I know Singaporeans are *kiasu*, but she has a legitimate concern since so many of our transactions are online. And these tech criminals are getting smarter and smarter each day. Do you know of any research on cybersecurity breaches?"

"Hey, friend. I'm a business professor. You can ask me about finance, economics, real estate – I can answer those. Technical computer stuff is out of my scope," was Sumit's reply. He was wondering why his friend Roy thinks he knows everything.

"But I can shed light on a research I did in India on cybersecurity breaches. I know the data is from India, but I think we can learn from them.

"Well, we studied three unexpected data breaches. The main one involved a food delivery company. The other two concerned an online grocery store and a bank."

Breach #1: Food Delivery Company

Sumit described, "The first organization is a leading food delivery company in India. The company has restaurants on its online platform and provides food ordering and delivery services from parent restaurants in select cities like Delhi, Mumbai, Bangalore and Kolkata. Customers can choose to pay by cash, digital wallet, credit card or internet banking.

"In the middle of Week 20 of that year, customer account information on the platform was discovered to have been sold on a dark web marketplace. It involved 17 million users' names, email addresses and passwords.

"The firm claimed that it had reset passwords for all affected users and logged them out of its app and website, and no payment information was leaked. Nonetheless, despite such assurances, users were still concerned about privacy issues. We are humans after all, and concerns about risks are to be expected when trust has been breached.

"Users were concerned about their payment information which would affect their willingness to use digital payment methods when ordering on this platform. They would also be concerned about their private information not related to payment matters, such as emails and residential addresses. If that is the case, this would affect whether they want to continue using the platform or not.

"We found that, after the breach occurred in the middle of Week 20, despite the firm's assurances, users switched from digital payments to cash payment. There was a sharp decline in the number of orders using digital payments immediately till the end of that week, while the order count for cash payments increased.

"But, what's interesting is that the decline in use of digital payment was

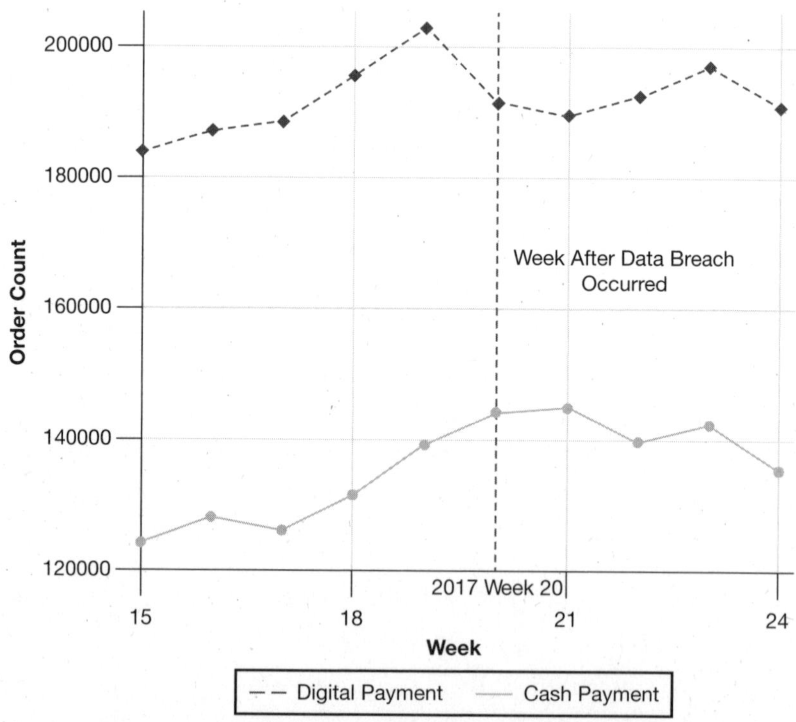

Payment Modes Before and After Data Breach (Short Term)

only temporary. Cash users gradually recovered and the gap between digital and cash payments widened. By Week 31, digital payments had recovered to the levels before the breach."

"Huh? Why did that happen?" asked Roy. "I would have thought that, with trust broken, users would be more cautious and used cash instead of digital payment."

[U]sers prefer convenience over privacy in the long run.

"Well," replied Sumit, "It meant that users prefer convenience over privacy in the long run. They brushed aside concerns about privacy because they value convenience more.

"In fact, the trade-off between convenience and privacy exists not only in the choice of payment mode but also in the adoption of the online ordering platform. Users can save time in searching, ordering and

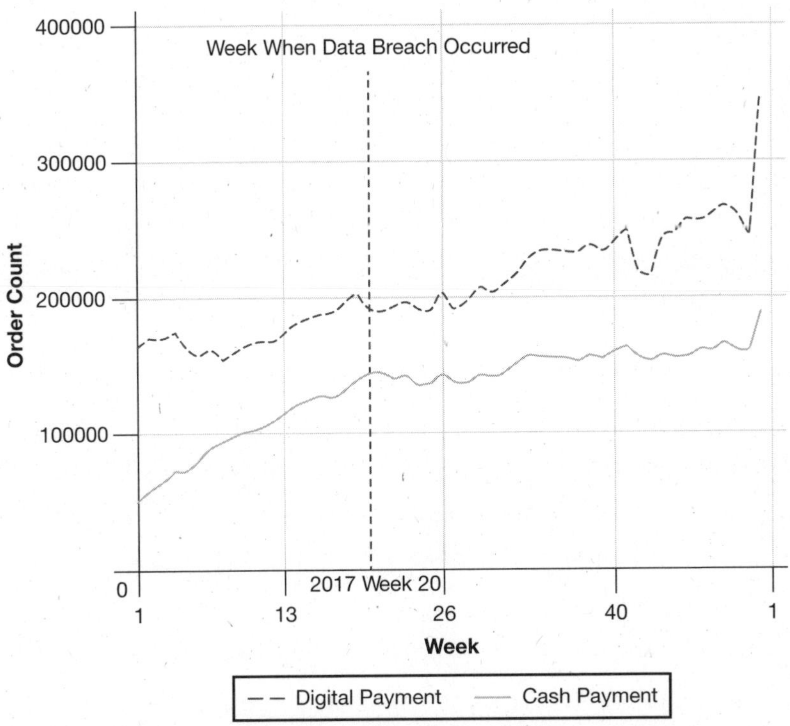

Payment Modes Before and After Data Breach (Long Term)

delivery using the platform. But they also run the risk of having their personal info exposed in the event of a leakage.

"We also studied whether the profile of users changed after the breach. We found no significant changes in the profile of customers who joined the platform after the breach.

"Even among users who quit... it appears the data breach had minimal impact on people's adoption of the food delivery platform. This reinforces our theory that consumers value convenience more than privacy," continued Sumit.

"Hmm... but among those who left the platform, did they vary in terms of whether they were digital payment users or cash users? I would think there would be more digital payment users dropping off than cash users," Roy mused.

"On the contrary, no," said Sumit, to Roy's surprise.

"Digital payment users preferred convenience and were reluctant to leave the platform; while cash users who preferred convenience less were more likely to quit the platform. Instead of immediately quitting, digital payment users sacrificed the convenience of digital platforms to secure payment privacy but still retained the convenience of the takeout ordering platform."

Breach #2: Online Grocery Store

"Let me get to the second company," continued Sumit. "We studied an online grocery store that experienced a data breach associated with a third-party login function. Hackers obtained access to login information and payment details from users who logged in via the Facebook third-party login function.

"We did the same set of tests as we did for the food delivery company. Just like the food delivery platform, we found only a mild decline in digital payments on the day of the data breach, with little change in sales. Also, the trend in the number of users who quit the grocery store after the breach did not change.

"We also found evidence that users switched from digital payment to cash payment. This means that, when they knew there was a breach, they adjusted their payments."

Breach #3: Bank

"Now, let's talk about the third data breach. This happened in a bank. The Indian banking system experienced a serious data breach that affected 3.25 million debit card users," said Sumit.

"Again, before and after the data breach, the changes in the transactions for both debit and credit cards were minor."

"Wow! Thanks, Sumit, for spending time to share your findings with me. I'll let Cal know. I think she's more old school and would favor cash over the convenience afforded by digital payments," said Roy.

WANT TO KNOW MORE?

This chapter is based on the following research:

Sumit Agarwal, Pulak Ghosh, Tianyue Ruan and Yunqi Zhang (2022), "Privacy versus Convenience: Customer Response to Data Breaches of Their Information," https://papers.ssrn.com/sol3/papers.cfm?abstract_id=3729730

19

CHAPTER

Illicit Wealth

"OMG! The property market is so hot," exclaimed Cal. "I can't believe that Singaporeans can afford to pay such high prices. Where do they get their money from?"

"I think one reason for the higher prices is foreigners who park their money here because their countries are not in good shape and Singapore is a safe country," Roy answered.

"Yeah, but still . . .," continued Cal. "I can't imagine people being so rich. I think we are both smart and work hard. How come we don't have the kind of money they have?"

These are questions that many Singaporeans ask themselves. What are some of the drivers of property prices?

Real Estate and Money Laundering

The real estate market has long been a prime destination for individuals seeking to launder illicit wealth. According to the Organisation for

Economic Co-operation and Development (OECD), money laundering through real estate is one of the oldest known ways to move and hide illicit funds. Because large amounts of money are used in one transaction, this activity is sometimes referred to as washing or laundering of funds.[1]

Countries including the United States, the United Kingdom, Australia, Canada and Germany are money laundering real estate hubs with London, Toronto, Vancouver and New York being hotspots. According to the Global Financial Integrity, more than $2.3 billion was laundered through the U.S. real estate from 2015 to 2021. A report by Transparency International showed that £1.5 billion of U.K. property – mostly in London – was bought by Russians accused of corruption. It found that over 2000 firms registered in the United Kingdom were used in 48 Russian money laundering and corruption cases. Together, these cases involved more than £82 billion worth of funds disguised by rigged procurement, embezzlement and bribery.

In Singapore, a money laundering case involving more than 110 properties and 62 vehicles worth over $1.24 billion was uncovered in 2023. The total value of assets seized or issued with prohibition of disposal orders amounted to more than $2.4 billion. Foreign nationals were behind the money laundering.[2]

There are adverse consequences from money laundering. Property prices may be artificially distorted. This makes it difficult for many people living in countries with rampant money laundering activities to afford housing. There is corruption. Money laundering usually goes hand in hand with drug trafficking, human trafficking, terrorism and other forms of organized crime.

Real estate is typically involved in the last phase of a money laundering

---

[1] "Understanding Money Laundering in Real Estate," https://complyadvantage.com/insights/real-estate-money-laundering/

[2] "Singapore Money Laundering Case Snowballs Further to over S$2.4 billion in Assets Seized or Frozen," *Channel News Asia*, 20 September 2023, https://www.channelnewsasia.com/singapore/billion-dollar-money-laundering-case-24-billion-assets-police-3785731

scheme. Illicit wealth is reinjected into the legal economy after going through a series of complex financial transfers created to disguise the financial assets and origins of their owners. These intricate financial transfers are usually made through corporate structures in offshore jurisdictions with strict bank secrecy, which are favored destinations for illegitimate wealth associated with fraud, embezzlement, bribery, tax evasion and money laundering.

The involvement of offshore vehicles in property purchases is not uncommon. According to Thomson Reuters and Transparency International UK, 91% of London properties owned by overseas companies were registered in secrecy havens, places that enable individuals to hide their wealth from the rule of law.[3]

Yet, given the unobservable and clandestine nature of illicit wealth, it is not easy to identify illegal real estate transactions. The United Nations reports that less than 1% of illicit wealth is ever detected, with this figure possibly being as low as 0.2%.

There are three stages in a money laundering process: placement, layering and integration. In the first stage, funds directly associated with crimes are placed in the financial system in different forms. The second stage involves the concealment of the criminal origin of proceeds, with offshore vehicles and their opaque ownership structures used for purposes of layering. Real estate often plays a role in the final stage, in which laundered illicit proceeds are integrated into the legal economy through investments.

The Panama Papers

"Have you heard of the Panama Papers?" asked Roy.

"Nope. I've only heard of the Panama Canal. What is Panama Papers about?" responded Cal.

3 "A Top Destination for Money Launderers," Thomson Reuters and Transparency International UK (2016).

"There is this Panama-based provider of offshore financial services called Mossack Fonseca & Co.," explained Roy. "Offshore financial services are sometimes used to conceal illicit wealth. In April 2016, there was a leak involving 214,000 offshore shell companies linked to people, including world political leaders and prominent business leaders, in more than 200 countries. Referred commonly to as the Panama Papers, the leaks showed, among other information, real estate transactions associated with offshore secrecy.

"Guess what? A study of the Panama Papers by NUS professors found that, of the 100,000 private property transactions in Singapore from 1995 to 2018 that contained buyer details, over 2300 of these involved buyers implicated by name in the Panama Papers."

"What? Such things can happen in Singapore?" gasped a disbelieving Cal. She had always thought Singapore is corrupt-free.

"Yup. These properties tended to be at the higher end of the property market where prices were higher, locations were more strategic and property characteristics such as floor level, property size and tenure were more highly valued," said Roy.

"Hah! That's why our property prices are high," said a somewhat upset Cal. "Who are these Panama-linked property buyers?"

Panama-linked Buyers

Singaporeans constitute the largest proportion of Panama-linked transactions, but their numbers have been declining drastically since 2010. In 2011, the number of Panama-linked Chinese buyers surpassed the numbers of Singaporean and Indonesian buyers for the first time. Since then, the number of Panama-linked transactions, regardless of buyer nationality, has been declining.

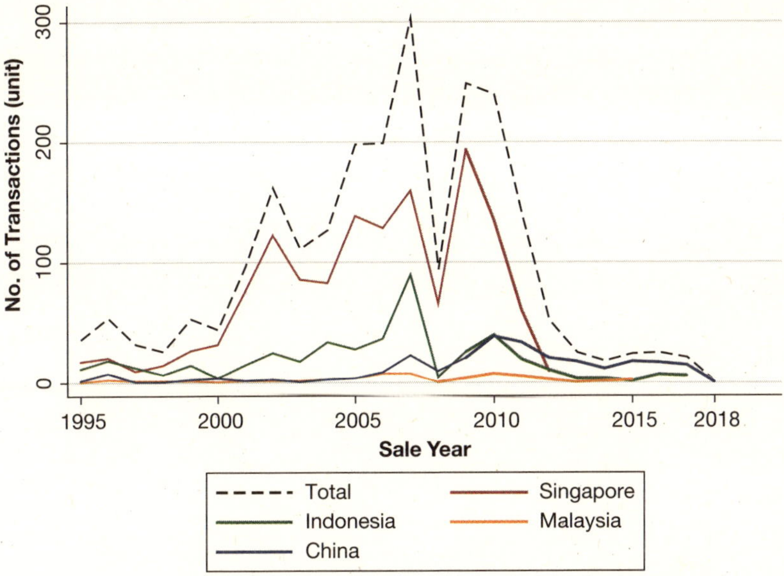

Number of Panama Transactions by Year and Buyer's Nationality

Panama Price Premium

"So what did the profs find in their study?" asked Cal. She was eager to know more. She thought this was juicy news that she could share with her friends.

"The profs compared these Panama buyers of Singapore properties with non-Panama buyers in terms of purchase price paid, and found that Panama-linked individuals pay, on average, a 3.7% premium for properties. Assuming a property is valued at $1.3 million, they would pay $50,000 more for that property. This Panama premium is likely to be an underestimation as not all buyers connected with illicit activities are captured in the Panama Papers."

"*Aiyoh*! Why are Panama-linked buyers willing to pay a higher property price?" enquired Cal.

With a straight face and a matter-of-fact tone, Roy explained, "First, Singapore is a safe haven. The Panama premium may well be due to buyers washing large sums of illegitimate proceeds through offshore vehicles. Given Singapore's political and economic stability, the property market is considered by many as a safe-haven investment destination. Thus, such buyers were willing to pay premiums to launder their ill-gotten wealth.

"Or, the premium may be purely due to Panama-linked buyers' high net worth and strong economic position which are not related to illicit financial flows or their connections to offshore corporations. This would be the wealth reason for the price premiums.

"But the NUS professors found that there is evidence indicating the safe-haven reason for the Panama premium and offshore secrecy."

Property Type

"So, did they buy the big landed properties?" asked a curious Cal as she recalled several good class bungalows had gone at record-breaking prices.

"Well, Panama-linked buyers tended to buy more expensive units in terms of both price per square foot and absolute transacted price," replied Roy. "The average transaction price is $1.8 million, about $500,000 higher than the average transacted price paid by non-Panama linked buyers. These individuals buy larger, newer properties located on higher floors. They purchase houses situated at more strategic locations. The properties are located closer to the Central Business District, within 6.5 km.

"Additionally, over 56% of the Panama-linked transactions involve freehold properties, which is more than 49% of the non-Panama-linked transactions.

"The purchased properties tend to have higher exclusivity. These property projects are small with fewer occupants. Moreover, Panama-linked buyers tend to have a shorter holding period and higher selling price per square foot."

"What does that mean?" asked Cal. These terms were getting too technical for her.

"Aahh . . .," explained Roy. "It means that Panama-linked buyers do not own the property for as long as non-Panama-linked buyers. They have a shorter holding period. But when they sell, they sell at a higher price per square foot. So, it seems like they know when to sell. They time their selling well."

Spillover Effects

Roy continued. "There was short-term neighborhood spillover effects of the Panama premiums. The profs found that the spillover effects were negligible in lower-end neighborhoods and primarily appeared in higher-end neighborhoods. In high-end neighborhoods, property prices rose by 3.5% after a Panama-linked transaction occurred nearby. "

Country and Corruption

"All this is due to corruption," said a disgruntled Cal. "I don't like this. Where do these buyers come from? I bet they come from countries that are corrupted."

"You're on the right track," smiled Roy. He then continued, "Countries vary in how attractive they are for criminal activities and money laundering. The NUS profs thought that buyers, whose home country is more corrupt or more easily exploited for criminal activities because of weak regulatory environment, are more likely to pay a higher premium.

"In general, there is a strong association between the premiums paid by buyers for a property and the level of corruption and money laundering in their home country. Buyers, whose home countries have the highest levels of corruption, pay a premium of 6.8%."

Wow!
I heard that there was a leak on money launderers.
And included in the list were some Singaporeans.
What do these money launderers do?
Tons of money are used in one transaction to wash dirty money.
Buying properties is a popular way to launder money.
And so property prices may be artificially distorted.
A study found that in Singapore, those identified in the money laundering leak paid almost 4% more for properties here.
And this is likely to be underestimated because not all money launderers were identified in the leak.
Oh . . .
I think Singapore's political and economic stability makes it a safe haven for such purchases.

These buyers buy expensive properties that are larger, newer, located at higher floor, and near CBD.
And I bet they don't hold on to these properties for long.

Also, if buyers come from a country that is corrupt, they tend to pay a higher premium for the property. These foreigners pay 3.7% more while locals involved in money laundering pay a smaller premium.
I think these foreigners buy penthouses and those with a better view.

Interestingly, about 1/3 of our local money-laundered-associated buyers are HDB upgraders. And not surprising, real estate agents make up a large proportion of buyers in these money-laundered-linked transactions.

"I know off-hand which are the corrupt countries. But surely, given that this was a university research, the profs must have used some measure of corruption?" asked Cal.

Roy nodded. "Using the Corruption Perception Index (CPI) from Transparency International to measure the home country's corruption, the professors found that a one-point lower average CPI value is associated with a 0.2% higher Panama premium. The lower the CPI, the more there is corruption. For example, an Indonesian buyer who has an average country CPI of 35, pays a 10% higher Panama premium than a Singaporean buyer who has an average country CPI of 85.

"A second measure of corruption is the bribery rate published by the Global Corruption Barometer. The rate indicates the percentage of people who reported paying a bribe in their dealings with a public service provider. The profs found that a 1% higher bribery rate in the home country translates to a 0.39% higher Panama premium on the property purchase."

Local vs Foreign Buyers

"What about the premium? Are there differences in the premium paid between local and foreign buyers?" asked Cal.

"There sure is. The average Panama premium is about 3.7% for foreigners, while that of locals is 3.4%," said Roy. "And do you know which foreign buyers pay the highest premium?

"The proportion of overpayment in Panama-linked transactions is larger among Indonesian buyers than among Chinese and Malaysian buyers. Further, transactions with a Panama premium are concentrated in the Central region where Indonesian buyers cluster."

"While it is understandable that foreigners benefit from using Singapore as a safe haven, how does it benefit Singaporeans to justify paying a premium?" asked Cal.

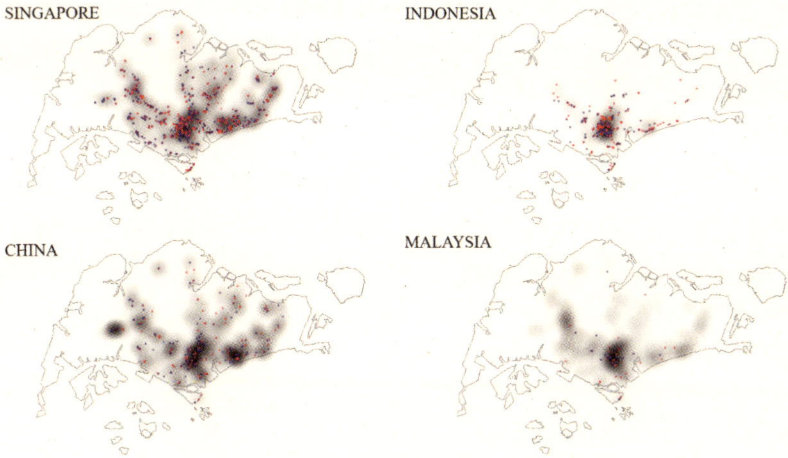

Distribution of Panama-linked Transactions by Overpayment Status and Buyer's Nationality

Note: The Panama-linked transactions, indicated by the red and blue dots, are overlaid on the black-white gradient heatmap that illustrates the concentration of non-Panama-linked transactions made by buyers of the same nationality. Red and blue dots represent Panama-linked transactions that are overpaid and underpaid, respectively.

"Well, according to the professors, a possible explanation could be that Panama-linked local buyers cherry-picked superior property units such as penthouses and those with a better view when purchasing properties. They found that Panama-linked locals were 3.9% more likely than other local buyers to buy these superior units. Panama-linked locals were 10% more likely to buy properties from sellers who were connected to the Panama Papers. Their purchase premium, vis-à-vis that of non-Panama-linked buyer-seller pairs, is 28.6% higher. This exceptionally large premium is suggestive of possible collusion among Panama-linked local individuals to manipulate property prices through such transactions," said Roy.

"Now, I want to know whether these Panama-linked buyers live in HDB flats," quizzed a mischievous Cal. She has seen numerous HDB dwellers driving big cars and always wondered why there appears to be contradiction between residence and other assets owned.

"Haha . . . the profs found that the proportion of HDB upgraders among Panama-linked local buyers was exceptionally high," said Roy with a smile as he saw Cal's face lit up. "Over one-third (35.4%) of these buyers were HDB upgraders – first-time buyers of private property who previously lived in subsidized public housing, and usually thought to have lower purchasing power and higher price sensitivity. Compared to other HDB upgraders, those who are connected to the Panama Papers purchased properties at a 1.5% higher price. Despite this purchase premium, this group of buyers was almost 5% less likely to obtain a mortgage and 6.6% less likely to use their Central Provident Fund savings for their property purchase."

"So this means that some Panama-linked local buyers might be straw buyers who purchased on behalf of third parties for various reasons," Cal surmised from Roy's explanations. "And a straw buyer may be employed if there are certain legal or financing restrictions preventing real buyers from making a property purchase in the local property market. Overpayments might explain the disguised buyers' willingness to pay for the properties."

Roy nodded in agreement.

"How about real estate agents?" Cal continued. "I'm always suspicious of them."

"The profs found that real estate agents constituted a large share of buyers in Panama-linked property transactions," responded Roy. "About 17% of the Panama-linked transactions involved buyers who were real estate agents, more than twice the figure of 7.5% of agent buyers in non-Panama-linked transactions."

[R]eal estate agents constituted a large share of buyers in Panama-linked property transactions.

"I can see why real estate agents end up being Panama-linked buyers," said Cal. "A real estate agent buyer has benefits. There are agent discounts that applied also to Panama-linked property transactions."

"You are right," nodded Roy as he marveled at how astute his wife is. "The professors found that real estate agents connected to the Panama Papers purchased properties at a 5.1% lower price than Panama-linked non-agent buyers. This discount not only neutralizes the Panama premium but also brings down the purchase price further by almost 1%. Additionally, Panama-linked agent-buyers were 8% more likely to hold their properties and obtained almost 6% higher gain when they decided to sell, vis-à-vis non-Panama-linked agent-buyers.

"Altogether, the findings suggested that real estate agents, as important gatekeepers of real estate transactions, were likely to be employed as straw buyers in property purchases. Their knowledge and experience in the local property market could help circumvent the legislation and obtain larger returns by purchasing at discounted prices and re-selling at higher prices."

Intervention

"Something must be done to curb these illegal activities," said Cal. "They drive up property prices and we are the ones who suffer."

"Well, a policy change was implemented to control cross-border cash movements," said Roy. "The Cross-Border Currency/Bearer Negotiable Instruments Reporting Regime (CBCRR) took effect on November 2007 which requires all persons carrying or posting cash or negotiable instruments of more than $30,000, or equivalent in foreign currency, into or out of Singapore to report to the Suspicious Transaction of Reporting Office (STRO). This policy change was aimed to deter cross-border movements of currency by cash couriers linked to money laundering and terrorism financing activities.

"Did this policy work?" asked an impatient Cal.

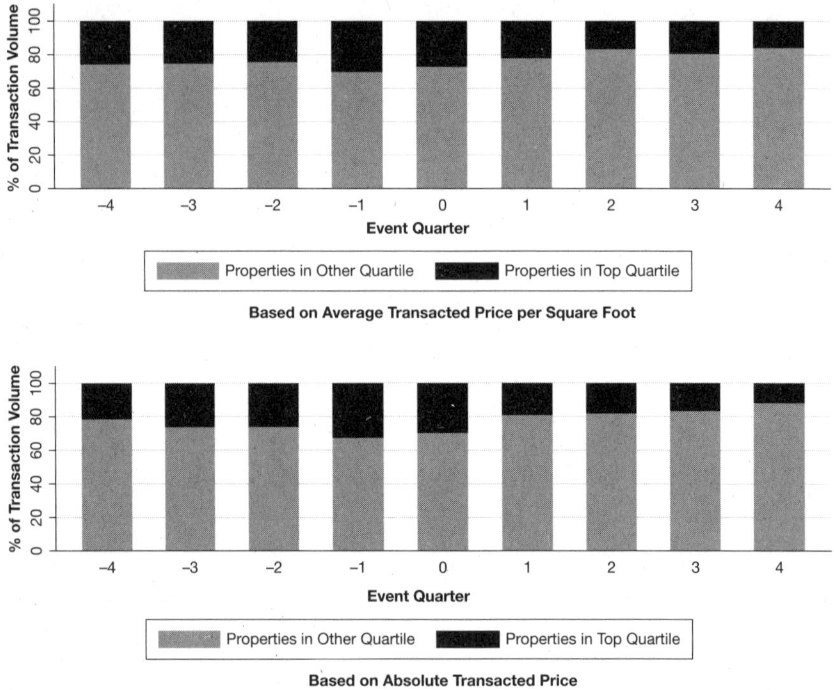

Transaction Volume by Property Segments
Pre- and Post-CBCRR Policy Implementation

Note: The figure shows the proportion of transaction volume by property segments. The time indicator in the horizontal axis is denoted as Event Quarter, it corresponds to the implementation of Cross-Border Currency/Bearer Negotiable Instruments Reporting Regime (CBCRR) policy on 1 November 2007. For instance, Event Quarter$_0$ comprises property transactions occurred within the three-month period after the policy was implemented, while Event Quarter$_{-1}$ comprises transactions occurred in the 3-month period before the policy introduction. Properties are categorized into five quartiles based on properties' average transacted price per square foot in developer sales (the upper panel), or properties' absolute transacted price (the bottom panel), with the top quartile containing properties in the highest-end segment (5th quartile).

"After the implementation of CBCRR, the transacted price of properties sold by Panama-linked individuals fell by 5.5% compared to that of properties sold by sellers with no Panama connections. The proportion of luxury properties transacted declined after CBCRR was instituted," explained Roy.

"Compared to the three months before CBCRR was implemented, the proportion of transactions involving properties in the top quartile declined by about 41% in the three months after the policy change. Panama-linked buyers bought properties at a lower price after CBCRR. Purchase prices were almost 4% lower three months after the policy introduction."

"Additionally, in November 2010, the Estate Agents (Estate Agency Work) Regulations (EAW) was implemented to enhance monitoring and regulatory oversight in the real estate market," continued Roy. "The regulation strengthened the gatekeeping role of the newly established Council of Estate Agencies (CEA), the regulator of real estates, salespeople and agencies, in real estate transactions.

"After the implementation of EAW, buyers stopped overpaying to avoid triggering a reporting threshold. Straw purchasing ceased. The year-over-year number of Panama-linked transactions decreased by 36% after the policy implementation and by 72% in the second year following the implementation."

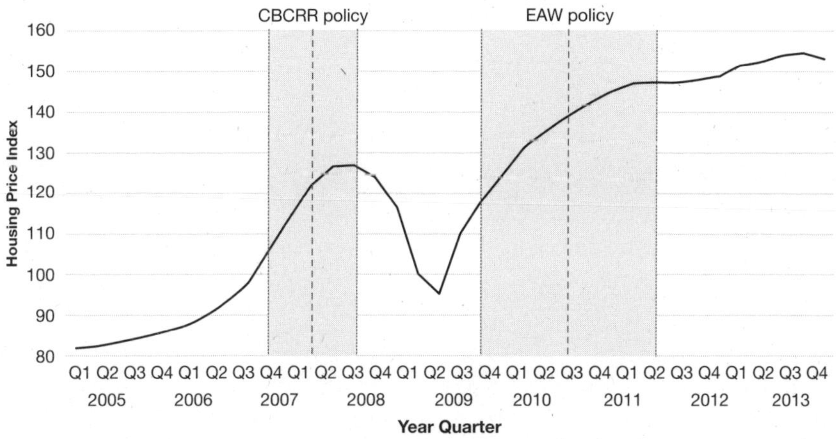

Singapore Housing Index

Note: The figure plots the housing price index obtained from Real Estate Information System (REALIS). The dotted vertical lines indicate the period during which the policies, namely Cross-Border Currency/Bearer Negotiable Instruments Reporting Regime (CBCRR) and Estate Agents (Estate Agency Work) Regulation (EAW), were introduced. The shaded time periods represent 1-year rolling window (6-months before and after) of CBCRR policy, and 2-year rolling window (1-year before and after) of EAW policy.

"Good!" said Cal as she heaved a sigh of relief. "Otherwise, we will have runaway property prices and many of us will not be able to own properties in our own country. But the case involving foreign nationals and over 100 properties and 60 vehicles shows that money laundering activities still exist."

WANT TO KNOW MORE?

This chapter is based on the following research:

Sumit Agarwal, Liu Ee Chia and Tien Foo Sing (2020), "Straw Purchase or Safe Haven? The Hidden Perils of Illicit Wealth in Property Markets", https://papers.ssrn.com/sol3/papers.cfm?abstract_id=3688752

CHAPTER 20

GST and Terrorist Attacks

"GST will be increased soon," Claire cautioned Lizzy. "We need to be careful with money. Buy only what we need. Occasionally, we can buy what we want to reward ourselves when we've achieved something. And switch to a cheaper brand if possible. We do not always have to buy the best brand."

"It's only a 1% increase, Mum," said Lizzy with a frown. "Why are you making such a big deal when the impact is so minimal," Lizzy shrugged.

Claire patiently explained what happened in India when the GST was introduced. Her husband, who goes on frequent business trips to India, had told her how Indian consumers responded when GST was introduced.

"People curbed their expenditure," he had said. "When there was an increase in GST, people reduced their spending. That was expected, but what was unexpected is that, for products with tax cuts, consumers also reduced their spending on such products."

GST Reform in India

The GST Reform in India was designed to create a unified tax regime across Indian states by unifying ranges of different indirect taxes into one tax that is collected at both the state and federal levels. It was announced in April 2017 and implemented in July of the same year. GST is levied on all transactions including sales, transfers, purchases, bartering, leases and import of goods and services. It merges central and state taxes into a five-tier schedule of 0%, 5%, 12%, 18% and 28%. Hence, some products experience a tax cut, some no change, and others a tax increase. Only petroleum products, alcoholic drinks and electricity are exempted from GST as they are taxed separately by the individual state governments.

The Supermarket Study

A study was conducted where the shopping behavior in 157 stores of a large Indian supermarket was observed.

In the months after the GST Reform was announced but not yet implemented, there was an increase in consumer's monthly purchases in anticipation of the tax increase. For every percentage point of tax increase for a product, consumers increased their spending by around 0.11%.

After GST was implemented, the study found that consumers reduced their monthly purchases when the product experienced an increase in tax rate. And vice versa. A 1% point increase in the tax rate led to a 0.48% reduction in spending, while consumers decreased their monthly purchases by almost 2% for tax cuts of the same magnitude. To be expected, the effect on spending was the strongest in the month immediately following GST implementation.

There was also evidence of a substitution effect. Substitution effect is the decrease in sales for a product that can be attributed to consumers switching to cheaper alternatives as its price rises. For example, when

Product A experiences a tax increase, consumers can switch to substitute products that serve the same purpose, and alter the relative consumption across products. Indian consumers were observed to buy cheaper brands given the price hike.

While consumers face higher prices when there was a rise in the tax rate, it was interesting that they did not appear to benefit when there were tax cuts as the final price for such products went up by 8.7 basis points. This suggests that merchants selling products that enjoy tax cuts also raised their prices, curbing people's spending.

"So, dear, we should be mindful of how we spend even though many people may consider the GST increase from 7% to 8% or 8% to 9% – only a 1% increase – to be marginal," said Claire as she tried to educate Lizzy on assessing financial matters in perspective.

"In reality, that is a 14% jump because it is 1% from a base of 7%. If you think about it that way, it is not as small as you think it is.

"And when GST goes up to 9%, that means more than a 28% increase because it is 2% from a base of 7%.

"But I understand why the increase in GST is needed. Singapore needs to fortify her reserves, especially after spending so much during the pandemic. Who knows what else lies ahead. That is why it is always prudent to have sufficient savings for use on a rainy day. This is true even at the personal level, so it applies to you and me too."

Terrorist Attacks

Rainy days means "a time in the future when money may be unexpectedly needed". This may be when a natural disaster occurs, such as the Chennai floods, or GST hike and inflation, or even wars and terrorist attacks.

Terrorist attacks increase uncertainty. And with uncertainty, people strategically adjust how they spend.

During times of uncertainty, the cost of using credit such as credit cards may go up. While spending on a credit card allows people to enjoy free credit for a certain period of time, excessive spending may result in the accumulation of high-interest revolving debt. So, future cost increases. At the same time, there are benefits of having access to assured credit, particularly crucial when the economy is uncertain.

So, how consumers adapt in their use of credit versus cash or debit card depends on their perception of how long they think the uncertainty will last, and how much weight they place on future costs.

If consumers expect the uncertainty to last a long time and place more emphasis on future costs, they may choose to be more conservative in how they spend and cut financing from credit accounts. On the other hand, if consumers expect the economic uncertainty to be short-lived, they may put more weight on the current benefits of access to credit and maximize on such credit access.

"Lizzy," said Claire. "You know Daddy goes to India quite often for business, right? Let me tell you something about India.

"India has experienced many terrorist attacks. Your Daddy told me that a group of researchers studied the effects on spending after a terrorist attack. Individuals and their spending from nine cities were studied. Five of these cities had experienced 31 terrorist attacks in a span of four years, while the other four cities did not experience any.

"The credit spending for both attacked and unattacked cities were similar before terrorist incursions, but this changed after an attack."

"How so, Mummy?" enquired Lizzy.

Claire replied. "Specifically, the daily credit card spending ratio of consumers in previously attacked cities increased by 0.2% more than consumers in the other cities.

"If the terrorist attack was more severe, the credit card spending ratio increase was driven more by consumers living in the same district as the hit location, and the attack resulted in people killed or wounded."

"I would think how spending is affected would be influenced by demographics," responded Lizzy as she remembered what she had learnt in Economics.

"Yes, you are right," replied her mum. "How people spent as a result of a terrorist attack varied depending on their demographic profile. Adjustments were more pronounced for men than women, and for those who were older, married or had longer tenures with the bank.

How people spent as a result of a terrorist attack varied depending on their demographic profile.

"Consumers with high liquidity constraints, like those with less than six months of bank balance, increased their credit card usage. Those who had revolving credit card debts also spent more on credit.

"The notion of liquidity is important. Remember how Dad and I have been telling you about being prudent and saving for a rainy day? Well, as the impact of economic uncertainty was less severe among individuals with stable cash flows, the increase in credit card spending ratio was found to be more prevalent among people who were not formally employed and hence, their cash flow was not stable.

"The researchers also observed there was a shift from debit account spending to credit account spending. But for people who do not have credit cards and hence no access to credit, their debit card usage did not vary."

"Wow, Mum," said Lizzy. "It looks like, when there's a terrorist attack, people just max out on their credit spending. Maybe they treat it like there is no tomorrow and so they just spend. I should just do the same if ever this happens in Singapore."

"Hey, you shouldn't think that way," Claire admonished.

"What if the attack was short-lived and everything went back to normal? Then, your increased credit spending would still have to be repaid. And if you cannot repay it and go into debt, the cost is very high. The interest rate on credit card debt is one of the highest, and it will just snowball. And not only that, your personal credit rating goes down and it will become hard for you to borrow in future."

"You know what, Mum?" said Lizzy. "I bet these two research studies will be useful for my upcoming Economics project. We have to demonstrate how economic principles like substitution effect and elasticity of demand can be applied in real-life settings. I think these studies fit in perfectly. Thanks, Mum."

WANT TO KNOW MORE?

This chapter is based on the following research:

Sumit Agarwal, Debarati Basu, Pulak Ghosh, Bhuvanesh Pareek and Jian Zhang (2019), "Tax-Pass-Through, Pricing Strategy and Consumer Spending Dynamics: The Indian GST Experience," https://www.researchgate.net/publication/334038694_Tax-Pass-through_Pricing_Strategy_and_Consumer_Spending_Dynamics_The_Indian_GST_Experience

Sumit Agarwal, Pulak Ghosh, Weiqiang Tan and Xin Zou (2023), "Terrorist Attacks and Strategic Household Consumption," https://papers.ssrn.com/sol3/papers.cfm?abstract_id=3754751

CHAPTER 21

Retirement Support Program

"Hello, Ma," Cal greeted her mother during their weekly phone call. Both her parents are retirees and live by themselves in a 3-room HDB flat. Her mother was a homemaker ever since Cal was born, while her father was a taxi driver. Since her mother had not worked for most of her life, her contribution to CPF was minimal. Her father's total contribution did not exceed $70,000.

Most countries face an aging population as birth rates decline and life expectancies extend. The global population aged 60 years or over numbered 962 million in 2017 and is expected to double by 2050.[1] The percentage of the population aged 65 and above is particularly high in developed countries. In Singapore, this age group will reach 47% by 2050. The sheer size of the elderly population exerts pressure on social security programs to meet retirement spending needs as some elderly

[1] United Nations (2017), *World Population Ageing 2017 – Highlights, Technical Report,* United Nations, Department of Economic Social Affairs, Population Division.

may not have sufficient savings to prepare for their extended life.

Policymakers have thus introduced support measures to alleviate retirement expenses. These support measures involve transfer programs where resources are directed to the needy in a speedy, effective and efficient manner. However, the transfer of such support can be challenging. For various reasons, some elderly over-spend, while others under-spend. Further, the elderly population is not homogeneous and the effectiveness of a transfer program may vary depending on the profile of different subgroups among the elderly.

In Singapore, there is a means-tested subsidy program targeted at low-income elderly Singaporeans. Called the Silver Support Scheme, elderly Singaporeans with limited pre-retirement cumulative income, limited current family support, and residential status in public housing (HDB) are eligible to receive quarterly subsidies from the government. The subsidies are not trivial. They range from $300 to $750 per individual per quarter, and are higher for people living in smaller HDB units. Those living in 1- and 2-room HDB flats receive $750, those in 3-room receive $600, 4-roomers get $450, and those in 5-room HDB flats are entitled to $300.

Cal's parents were entitled to $750 each, to be received every quarter as part of the support scheme.

"Have you had your lunch? When is your next check-up for your high blood pressure?" Cal asked.

"*Makan* already," replied Ma. "You *leh*? Must eat well. Eat nutritious food. Don't anyhow eat outside food. And now there are all these delivery services. *Alamak*! The food is oily and there's too much salt and MSG.

"You and Roy must come over for dinner more often. I cook for you. Homecooked food is the best. Don't worry about coming over for dinner. Although prices have gone up, I can still buy more groceries because I have more money!"

"How did you have more money? Is it the subsidy from the government?"

"Yes. My POSB account was credited already with $750 last week. Your Papa's also," said a happy Ma.

"Ma, the government gives you and Papa the money for your old age. It's for you to buy things you need because you are retired. It's not for you to anyhow spend," cautioned Cal.

"*Aiyah*! You think I don't know *meh*. You think I anyhow spend *meh*? But government gives us the money, we spend *lah*. We want to eat well. Things that we didn't dare to buy before because we were short of cash, we can now buy with the subsidy," said Ma. "In fact, I think Papa and I spend more than we usually do. We didn't even realize it."

"Huh? Ma, how much did you spend?" said a surprised Cal.

"Oh! The other day, your Papa was calculating how much we spend," said Ma. "Last time, for all our monthly expenses including electricity, water, conservancy, food and transport, and sometimes a little bit of shopping, we spend about $1400 each. That works out to about $47 a day.

"Then, the government started giving us $750 each, every 3 months. We started to buy better food, buy more snacks, and sometimes take taxi instead of the bus. Your Papa calculated that our expenses have gone up by more than $14 every day, and that's for the two of us together. Last time, it was $47 a day. Now, we spend more than $54 a day for each of us."

"*Aiyoh*, Ma. You think you're only spending $7 more each day, but it works out to 16% of what you used to spend before the government gave you the subsidy," said a shocked Cal as she worked out the numbers on her phone calculator.

"Did you spend all the money all at once?"

"Umm, almost all the money, I'm afraid. The money is there, what. By the end of the week, we spent almost half of the subsidy already. I didn't even realize how much we had spent," said Ma defensively.

"This is our fourth subsidy already. When we received the subsidy the first time, we were quite cautious and didn't dare to spend it. But, now, we know it'll always come every 3 months, so we'd just spend. We need to buy food and pay our bills. So, the subsidy comes in handy to cover such expenses."

Cal shook her head as she heard what Ma said. She understands that people differ in how much cash they have. Those with low liquidity or more cash constraints will tend to spend more in response to the subsidy. On the other hand, senior citizens who have more liquidity, are in less dire need to use the subsidy. Those with more liquidity constraints will use the subsidy funding more quickly to cover the cost of essential items. However, the increase in spending of $7 per day for three months for each person exceeds the $750 subsidy given. So with the subsidy, her parents are spending instead of saving more.

Cal made a mental note that she has to educate her parents on being more cautious with the money they have. While the government has been generous with these subsidies and her parents want to enjoy the rest of their lives, they shouldn't be overspending. Perhaps she should impose forced savings – a fraction of the subsidy to be saved each time there is a payment.

She thought how poetic that life has come full circle. When she was young, her parents would endlessly drum into her about being careful with her pocket money and even pushed her to cultivate the habit of saving 20% of her pocket money. Now, it seems like it would be her turn to educate her parents.

"Ma, on my next visit, I'll teach you how to better manage the subsidy, OK?" said Cal as she ended her call with her mother.

WANT TO KNOW MORE?

This chapter is based on the following research:

Sumit Agarwal, Wenlan Qian, Tianyue Ruan and Bernard Yin Yeung (2020), "Supporting Seniors: How Low-Income Elderly Individuals Respond to a Retirement Support Program," https://papers.ssrn.com/sol3/papers.cfm?abstract_id=3611637

Cal, do you know how much we spend each month on utilities, food and so on?
$1400 per person! That works out to $47 a day. Wow! I cannot imagine living costs to be so high.
That's why the government gives retirees like you and Papa money for your expenses.
Last week, we received $750 in our bank account. We're so happy. We spent half of it already. With the subsidy, our daily expenses is now $54 daily.
Aiyoh, Ma. That $7 increase is 16% more than your usual expenses.
But we don't have much savings. If we have, then we don't need to use much of the subsidy. The subsidy helps us to enjoy and eat better, and sometimes take taxi instead of the bus. Those with more cash will use less of the subsidy money, but for us, we use almost all of it.